PATRICE DARD

Photography
RAY WILSON and DANIEL CZAP

PATRICE DARD

MICRO WAVE COOKING

Photography
RAY WILSON and DANIEL CZAP

- **An all-embracing book** designed to be used with any and all models of microwave ovens, and for households large and small.
- **Advice**, tips and tricks for getting the most out of your microwave.
- Easy reference **charts** for information about cooking and defrosting.
- **Recipes** that are simple to follow, quick to prepare and delicious; with step-by-step instructions.
- More than **600** mouth-watering full-color **photos**.
- **Answers** to all the questions you are likely to have concerning microwaves and their use.

Brimar Publishing

Concept, execution of recipes and writing:
Patrice Dard

Photography:
Ray Wilson
and
Daniel Czap

Culinary Design Coordination:
Sophie Dard

Graphic Design:
René Barsalo for
Barsalo & associés

BRIMAR PUBLISHING INC.
8925 Saint-Laurent Boulevard
Montreal, Canada H2N 1M5
Telephone: (514) 384-8660
Telex: 05-826756

Legal deposit: Fourth Quarter 1986
Bibliothèque nationale du Québec
National Library of Canada

ISBN: 2-920845-06-3

Printed and bound in Canada

2001-A
2 3 4 5 6 7 8 9

INTRODUCTION

The fork is most definitely a multi-purpose tool. We are constantly reaching for one, whether to stab a succulent mouthful, anchor a piece of meat for cutting, roll up a forkful of spaghetti, beat eggs or whip a sauce smooth.

But would anyone actually consider using one to eat soup?

The microwave oven, one of the greatest inventions of modern times, has a good deal in common with the reliable old fork; we can expect a lot from it, but not everything.

First of all, we have to realize that a microwave does much more than a conventional oven; it performs many of the roles of the stovetop burner. You can use it to fry, sauté, boil, stew, simmer and reheat a variety of recipes including delicate sauces; you can even use it to cook or heat frozen foods.

And it performs all these roles quickly, cleanly, and without stacks of pots and pans to clean afterwards.

All these qualities have made the microwave oven an indispensable piece of equipment in today's kitchen.

But we would be dishonest if we did not admit that microwave ovens also have limitations, the most important of which is a fairly limited capacity.

Given the present state of technology, it is virtually impossible to produce, at a reasonable price, a microwave that can hold more than six portions at once.

And even for cooking for six, the microwave really cannot compete with the conventional oven. But if you are cooking single servings or for two or three, the microwave is the hands-down winner.

The second limitation of microwave cooking is also connected to its technical design. Basically, microwaves can raise the temperature of foods, but the air within the oven does not heat.

However, it is precisely that hot air inside a conventional oven which is responsible for browning the surface of a roast or turning a crust golden.

As a result, foods that require searing or browning do not turn out very well when cooked in the microwave, unless you use a few special techniques which we will discuss later.

Now that we have explained its limitations, we want to explore further some of the wonderful possibilities that microwave cooking offers.

But first, we want to mention that this book is more than an ordinary cookbook. It is the result of 15 years of culinary experience (in front of the stove or with pen in hand), and of nearly a full year of research on the specific use of microwave ovens.

Ray Wilson and Daniel Czap, both well-known specialists in food photography, spent months in our kitchen faithfully and devotedly recording the results of our work with their camera equipement.

The end product of this long collaboration between the "hand of the chef" and the "photographer's eye" is the collection of 600 stunning photographs in this book. The photos have been conceived to illustrate all the special techniques of microwave cooking, as well as to show the step-by-step preparation of numerous recipes, in order to eliminate any chance of error.

Even though we have presented a wide variety of recipes, they are all fast and simple to execute, because truly good cuisine is always simple.

Besides, microwave ovens are not really appropriate for long and complicated recipes; time and energy savings are the main virtues of microwaves.

Finally, we want to stress that in the preparation of this book we have been scrupulously honest about the results of our recipe experiments, so that the reader can benefit from all the special tricks and techniques we discovered.

We have described the pitfalls to avoid, and the disappointments and accidents that occur if you don't follow certain basic rules.

We have also made it a point of honor to present healthy and natural recipes, and to reconcile the art of gourmet dining with sound dietary principles. That is why each recipe includes information about calorie and fat content. For the same reason, we have recommended minimum amounts of salt in the recipes (which you can of course adjust to your personal taste).

Finally, we have given cooking times for different types of microwave ovens (based on their power capacity) and for different portions, to spare our readers the tedious task of conversion.

Here, then, is the first cookbook to present a comprehensive view of the art of microwave cooking.

Patrice Dard

Table of contents

The Microwave Oven

Cookware

Advice, Tricks and Secrets

Entrées

Fish, Shellfish and Crustaceans

Poultry

Meats

Vegetables

Desserts

The Microwave Oven

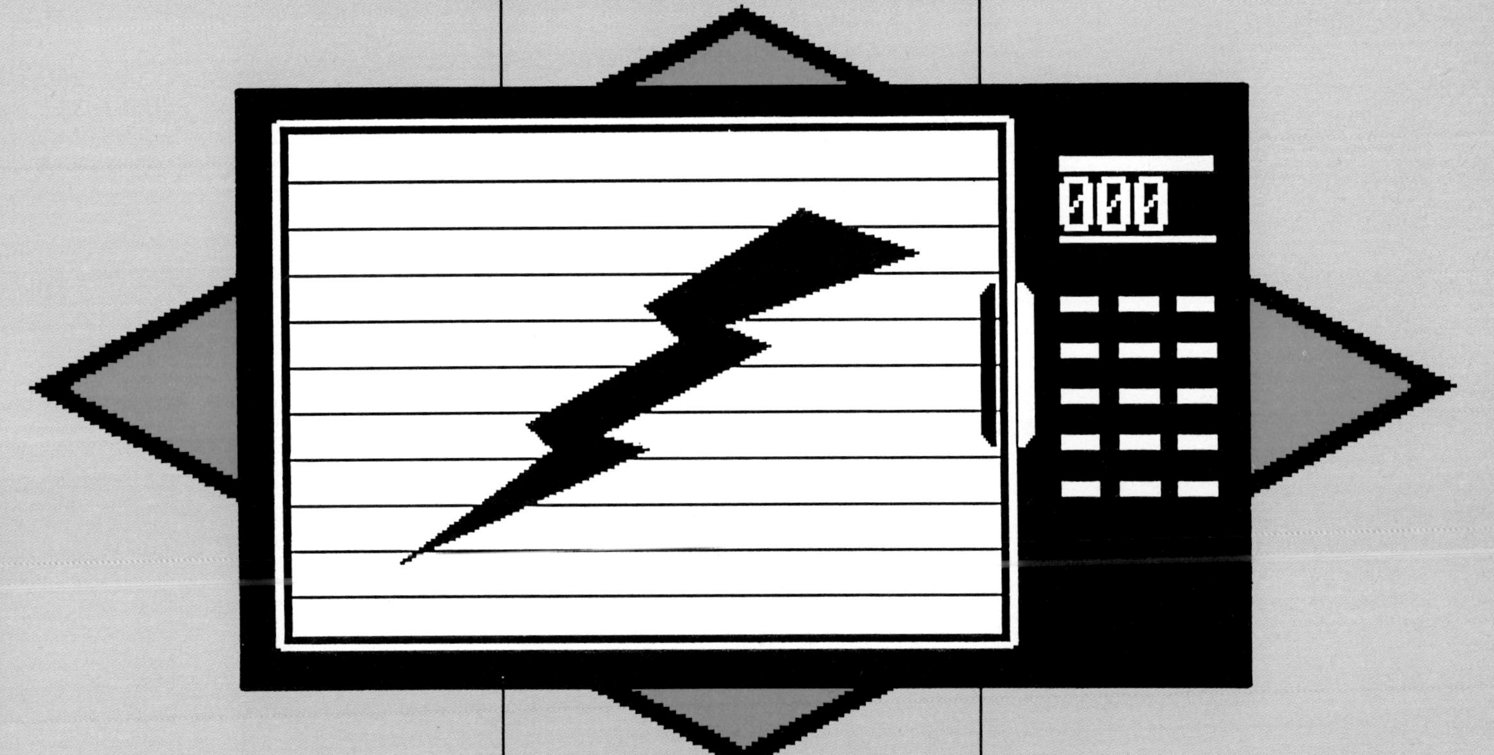

The Microwave Oven

Exactly what are microwaves?
Microwaves are a form of electromagnetic energy, naturally occuring in the universe. The waves are very short (thus the term "micro" waves), but have an extremely high frequency (2,450 radio waves). In other words, these waves oscillate at the rate of 2 billion times per second.

When closed, a microwave oven vaguely resembles a television set. This is not entirely accidental as both appliances function on the same basic principle: wave transmission. The television converts certain waves into pictures while the oven harnesses other waves to heat food.

How are microwaves produced?
They are produced by a generator, or *magnetron*, inside the oven. The magnetron transforms electric current into electromagnetic energy.
A *wave guide* distributes the microwaves in the oven as evenly as possible; the pattern of distribution varies with the manufacturer.

How do microwaves work?
They operate in three ways: By *absorption*, by *transmission*, and by *reflection*. Microwaves are attracted by moisture, which makes up 65% to 90% of foods. Water molecules in food absorb the waves. Certain materials such as paper, glass or plastic are transparent to the microwaves, in the same manner that window panes are to the sun. These materials, which neither absorb nor reflect the waves, allow them to directly penetrate foods (transmission). On the other hand, metal reflects the waves; so the metal walls of a microwave oven contribute to the best possible distribution of energy.

How is food cooked?
Each molecule of food subjected to microwaves oscillates more than 2 billion times per second, causing friction. The resulting heat cooks the food. Our forefathers used a similar principle when they rubbed two sticks together to produce fire.

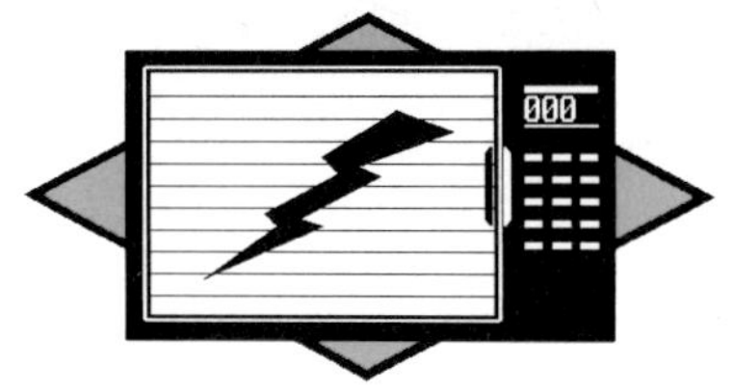

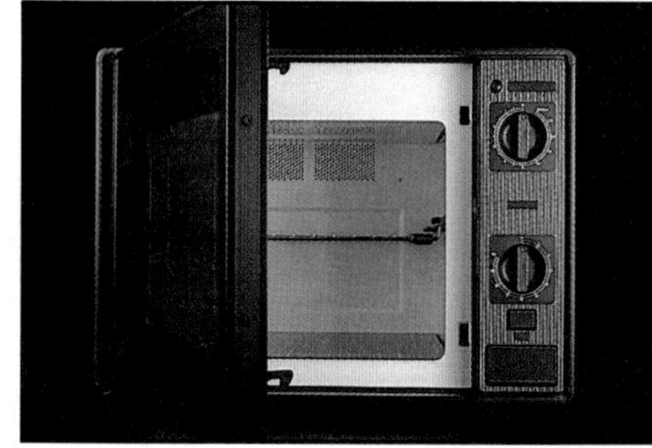

The walls of a microwave oven have been carefully constructed to prevent any waves from escaping. The magnetron also stops automatically and instantly when the door of the oven is opened. Therefore, there is ABSOLUTELY NO DANGER OF RADIATION. In addition, when the oven is stopped, no electromagnetic energy remains in the food.

The Hearth and the Shelf

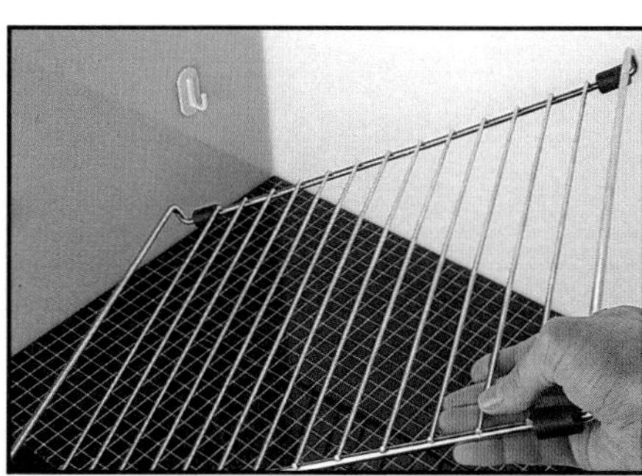

The bottom of the oven is lined with a thick glass plate which is usually removable: it is called a hearth. This element insulates the food from the bottom of the oven, allowing it to cook more evenly. Many ovens are equipped with a lattice-like shelf which forms a second cooking level; making it possible to cook two portions of a meal or two separate recipes at the same time.

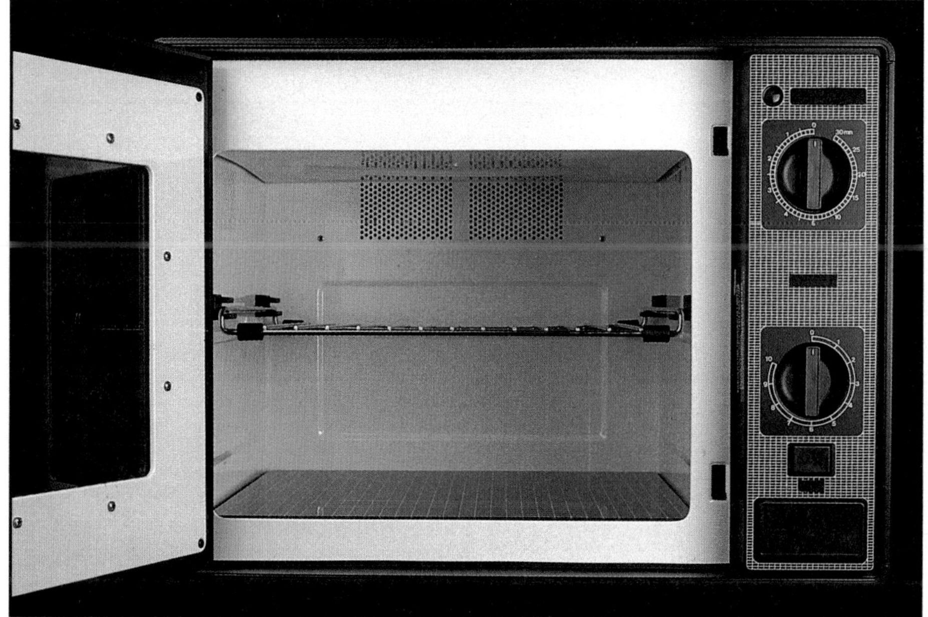

Unlike a conventional oven, the air in a microwave oven does not heat up. Since containers suitable for microwave use only heat up slightly, it is possible to handle them without fear of burns. However, be careful not to touch the metal walls of the oven.

The Timer

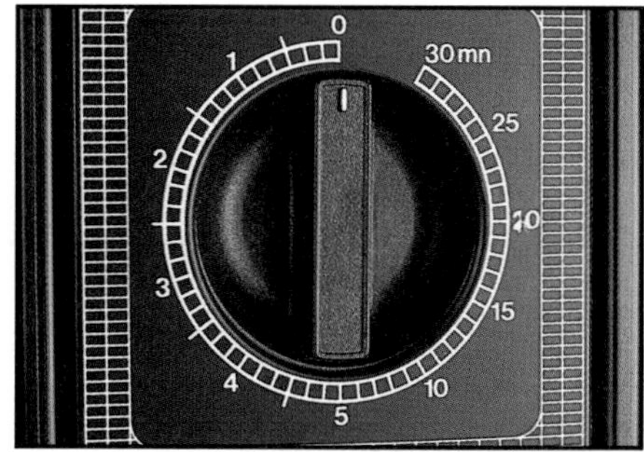

All microwave ovens are equipped with a timer. A variety are available: minute-timers, minute-timers / second-timers, numerical timers, etc. Their purpose is essentially to allow for precise programming of cooking time, to set off an alarm mechanism at the end of the cooking process and to automatically turn off the appliance.

Does The Microwave Oven Really Cook Foods Faster Than a Conventional Oven?

Absolutely! Cooking in a microwave oven is two to three times faster than the conventional method, depending on the type of food cooked. However, the microwave oven's efficiency is reduced when large quantities of food are cooked at once.

Microwave Oven Power

A microwave oven puts out only about half as much power as it consumes. For example, an oven which uses 1,350 watts only puts out 700 watts. The rest of the power is lost in the process of converting electricity to electromagnetic waves. But this loss of power is compensated for by the saving in time.

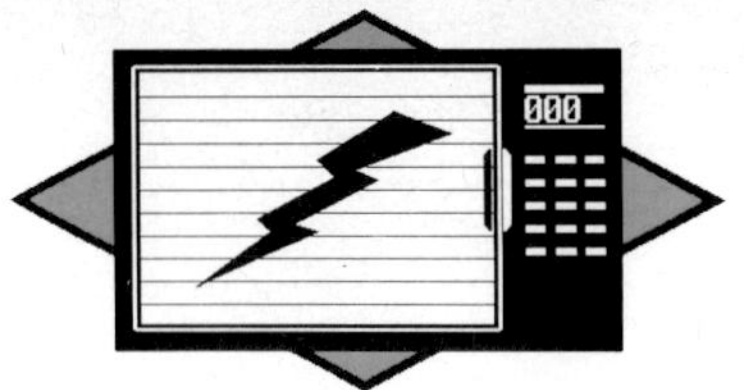

Is Microwave Cooking Economical?

A great number of tests have shown that the microwave oven and a conventional burner consume approximately the same amount of energy. However, the microwave oven uses about 70% less energy than a conventional oven.

What are the Most Common Power Levels of Microwave Ovens?

For domestic use, manufacturers build ovens of 500, 600, 650 and 700 watts. These figures refer to the maximum power of the appliance.

How Do You Adjust Cooking Time for the Power of your Microwave Oven?

First of all, establish the power wattage of your oven, and match it to the color-coded power level on the following chart:

500 watts
600/650 watts
700 watts

Once you have determined the color code for your appliance, match it to the appropriate cooking time for each recipe.

Power Setting

Microwave ovens may be programmed to put out power ranging from zero to the maximum capacity of the appliance. The level of power used at any given moment is called the *power setting*. The combination of timing and power setting controls cooking.

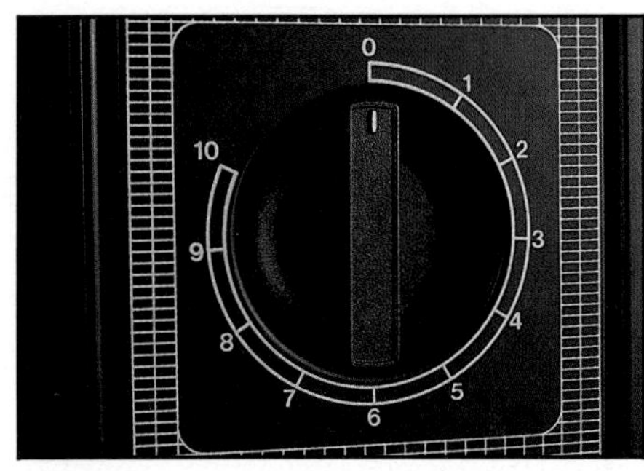

Microwave ovens are equipped with a control which permits various power settings. Some models offer only four or five settings, but most have 10.

What are the Most Common Power Settings?

Although most ovens have 10 different power settings, only four are frequently used:

HIGH: 100% power
Mode 10: Used for most cooking processes
MEDIUM-HIGH: 80% power
Mode 8: Used for the end of the cooking process
MEDIUM: 50% power
Mode 5: Used for gentle cooking
LOW: 30% power
Mode 3: For defrosting

(The "VERY LOW" setting, mode 1 or 10% power, is used to keep foods warm without further cooking.)

Latest Innovations

Technology is constantly improving, and each year, the consumer is presented with more sophisticated microwave ovens.

There are now microwave ovens on the market equipped with some of the elements of conventional ovens, such as grills, and convection (hot air) systems which permit browning. However, these additions limit the choice of cookware: a grill tends to burn paper, and plastic melts at high temperatures.

In addition, developments in programming systems permit some ovens to be programmed to start cooking at a designated time, adjust power settings, and end the cooking process all without the user being present. Some microwave ovens are actually mini cooking computers.

Based on the idea of "doing the most with the least," and because most families own a "standard" microwave oven, the recipes in this book have been designed to work in the simplest models, as long as they have a timer and variable power settings.

Those of you who are equipped with ultra-sophisticated models can try one of our recipes by following our guidelines and then according to manufacturer's guidelines. The comparison should prove interesting...

Cookware

Cookware

What are the important characteristics of utensils used for microwave cooking?
The ideal utensil for use in the microwave must be capable of transmitting waves into the food without absorbing or reflecting them.

The utensil which meets these requirements will cook more rapidly and save time and energy. As it does not retain heat, it will be easier to pick up and carry to the table for serving; thus less manipulation, and fewer dishes to wash.

Since the cooking utensil can also be used as a serving dish, its esthetic quality is a major consideration.

Are there many differences in the efficiency of various types of cookware?
Many! That is why we have grouped them into the following categories, according to the material from which they are made:

Forbidden materials
Materials to avoid
Materials that require testing
Acceptable materials
Materials to be used with caution
Ideal materials.

Forbidden Materials

As we noted earlier, metal reflects waves. This interferes with the uniform cooking of foods, but even worse, it causes microwaves to bounce around in erratic patterns inside the oven. These 'wild' microwaves can attack the metal lining of the oven and cause serious damage. Never use metal pots, frying pans, plates, moulds, lids or aluminum containers in your microwave oven. Aluminum foil should also be avoided, except in specific circumstances (see page 21). Melamine or Centura® brand products are also on the "not to be used" list.

Materials to Avoid

It is a good idea to avoid using any container which contains metal parts no matter how small. This includes: metal pot handles, metal skewers, glassware containing lead, delicate crystal, porcelain (especially if it has gold or silver decoration), and finally, thick wood cutting boards (in the long run, they split under the power of the microwaves).

Materials That Require Testing

Pottery, earthenware, ceramic and clay containers must first be tested before use in a microwave. Since many of them contain a certain amount of metal, they may or may not be suitable for microwave use.

Test

Pour a cup of water into the container to be tested and an equal amount in a microwave-safe container. Place both containers in the oven. Set the timer on HIGH (Setting no. 10).

First test: If the water starts to boil at the same time in both containers, the test result is positive. The container is microwave-safe.

Second Test: If the boiling process is not simultaneous, touch both containers. If the container being tested is no warmer than the microwave-safe container, it may be used. However, if it is too hot to touch while the latter is still cool, do not use it.

Materials to be Used with Caution

Cardboard (plates, glasses, cups, packaging) may be used in a microwave oven mainly to reheat foods. Do not heat it for long periods, especially if it contains fatty or heavily sweetened foods. When reheating food in a cardboard package, make sure that the package is not lined with aluminum. Paper towels and napkins may also be used for microwave cooking, but colored paper should be avoided as the color may run onto the food.

Most wicker, bamboo, rattan baskets and steamers can easily tolerate microwaves but only for short periods. The same holds true for wooden skewers and other small wooden instruments.

Any thin or pliable plastic cookware can be used in the microwave as long as it is not empty or used for a long period. Avoid using then to cook fatty foods or foods high in sugar content. They might become discolored, lose their shape or melt as sugar and fat reach extremely high temperatures very quickly.

Acceptable Materials

Containers made of tempered glass (Pyrex®), or tempered ceramic (of the Corning Ware® or Arcopal® type) are well suited to microwave cooking even though they may be somewhat heavier or more delicate than other containers. However, the plastic lids of these containers should not be used.

Ideal Materials

The hard plastic cookware specifically designed for microwave use is especially practical. It is not particularly cheap, but its durability and staying power far outweigh the initial expense. It is available in all shapes and sizes. Moreover, these dishes are attractively designed and can easily be brought directly from the oven to the table. They should not be used in the microwave when they are empty.

Size and Shape of Cooking Utensils

The manufacturers of microwave cooking utensils have displayed such ingeniousness and expertise in their bid to outdo one another that we now have a varied choice of cooking utensils; they come in all shapes and sizes, and are as attractive as they are practical. The most practical of all are those which to directly from the freezer (protected by a freezer lid) to the microwave oven (covered with a cooking lid) to the table as a serving dish.

Although it is not necessary to own every utensil on the market, you should equip your kitchen with a complete set of microwave cookware.

The appropriate utensil makes cooking easier and greatly contributes to the success of the recipe. Remember the old saying: "You know a true craftsman by the tools he uses".

Here then are a few utensils which are particularly useful for microwave cooking; we used them frequently to test the recipes in this book.

Three round dishes of the same diameter but different depths (diameter: 10 inches or 25 cm; capacity: 1 quart or 1 litre size, 2 quarts or 2 litre size, 3 quarts or 3 litre size). A single cooking lid serves for all three utensils.

Two rectangular, shallow dishes (Size: 12 in x 8 in x 2 in or 30 cm x 20 cm x 5 cm; 8 in x 5 in x 2 in or 20 cm x 13 cm x 5 cm. Capacity: 1 1/2 quarts or 1,5 litres and 1/2 quarts or 0,5 litre. The lid of the 1 inch deep oval dish (3 cm) doubles as a container for preparing recipes au gratin.

A deep rectangular dish (Size: 11 in x 6 in x 4 in or 28 cm x 15 cm x 10 cm; capacity: 2 quarts or 2 litres. A medium-deep round dish (diameter: 7 in or 18 cm; depth: 5 in or 12 cm; capacity: 1 1/2 quarts or 1,5 litres). Four small, square individual ramekins (Size: 4 in x 4 in x 2 in or 10 cm x 10 cm x 5 cm; capacity: 6 oz. or 200 ml). Each of these dishes comes with its own cover.

Three deep round pyrex casseroles (capacity: 1/2 quart or 0,5 litre; 2 quarts or 2 litres; 3 quarts or 3 litres). Their lids may be used for gratin dishes.

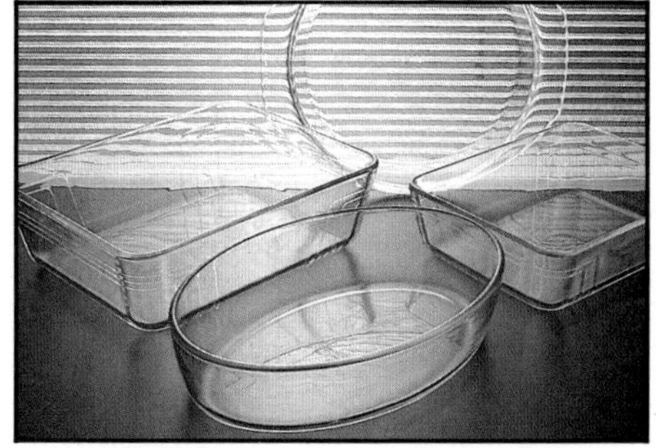

Two rectangular pyrex gratin dish (capacity: 1/2 quart or 0,5 litre). An oval pyrex gratin dish (capacity: 1 quart or 1 litre).

Warning: The freezer lids that come with some microwave dishes cannot be used in the microwave oven.

Remember that in a microwave oven, cooking time is faster and more uniform in a round dish than it is in a square or rectangular dish of the same capacity and depth. Food in the corners of a square-shaped, tends to overcook.

Special cookware

In addition to the containers described above, certain special utensils will add to your microwave cooking repertoire.

A few pie plates, tart plates, cake molds, savarin or charlotte molds, a measuring cup as well as two or three mixing bowls will all become vital equipment, along with a few utensils that may be unfamiliar.

What Are These Special Utensils?
There are quite a few. For example:

A cooking dish with a plastic grid on top is especially handy...

... particularly for steaming vegetables and other foods.

The trivet is designed especially to cook meats.

The raised grills allow meat and fowl to cook without stewing in their own juices. The drippings are easily collected. Dishes prepared on a grill are both tastier and healthier.

A divided cooking dish is a practical utensil to have on hand for microwave cooking. It can be used to warm two different side dishes at once...

... or to cook one vegetable with two different seasonings. On the left: For a guest on a low-salt diet.

On the left: For a child who does not like pepper.

On the left: For a husband who is watching his fat intake.

On the left: No diet restricts the use of herbal seasonings!

Browning dishes

We have already stressed the fact that one of the few limitations of microwave cooking that it cannot brown foods.

A number of manufacturers have designed special microwave browning dishes especially for this purpose.

How does the Browning Dish work?

The browning plate is specially designed to grill items such as steak, burgers, and chicken. For best results, place the empty dish in the microwave oven and preheat it for 6 minutes at maximum power (HIGH). Do not exceed the time limit and be sure to use oven mitts when removing the dish as it will be extremely hot.

Set the pieces of meat on the browning plate and fry quickly for 1 or 2 minutes, again on HIGH; turn the pieces over to brown the other side. You can finish cooking simple grilled dishes directly on the browning plate, or transfer the meat to another dish for more elaborate recipes.

When should you use a Browning Plate?

The browning plate is indispensable for preparing a beautiful golden chicken or roast beef in a microwave oven alone. It is also an ideal dish to use to reheat pizza, toast a sandwich or cook an omelet.

Set the empty plate in the bottom of the oven and preheat the dish at maximum power (HIGH) for 6 minutes.

Never preheat the browning plate on the microwave oven shelf or with its cover on. The browning plate in the above photo will not perform as it is designed to.

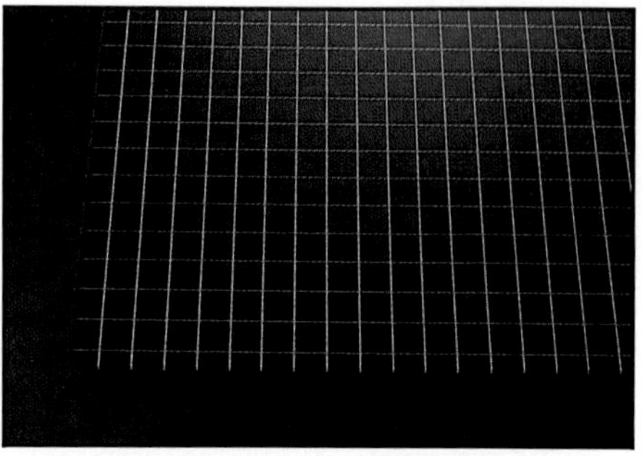

It is also better to pull out the glass bottom shelf of the oven, if it is removable, and preheat the browning dish directly on the metal base of the oven.

Once the dish is well heated, it can be used with or without fat or grease.

Press the food to be browned against the bottom of the plate. Roast or grill according to the specific recipe instructions.

Turn the meat over to brown all sides evenly.

What Special Care Does the Browning Plate Require?

- Never preheat the plate more than 8 minutes.
- Never handle the dish without oven mitts. Its temperature can reach upwards of 480° F. (250° C).
- Wash it by hand. Do not put it in the dishwasher, and never immerse it in water.
- Handle it with care; it is relatively fragile.

Plastic and paper products

Plastic and paper products are useful for many cooking processes but are especially well suited to microwave cooking.

Can You Use All Plastics and Paper Products?

Definitely not! You should use only those materials especially designed for kitchen or microwave use.

Many paper products and paper bags are unsuitable for microwave use because they are recycled paper products and may contain tiny metal fragments. Some plastic freezer bags also should not be used in the microwave as they can give off an odor that may affect the flavor of the food.

Wax paper and paper towels are choice materials in some instances (see page 16). Polyethylene plastic wrap and plastic cooking pouches may also be very practical. Never close plastic with metal ties. They might cause sparks to fly inside the oven and make the plastic melt. Regular string is a better choice.

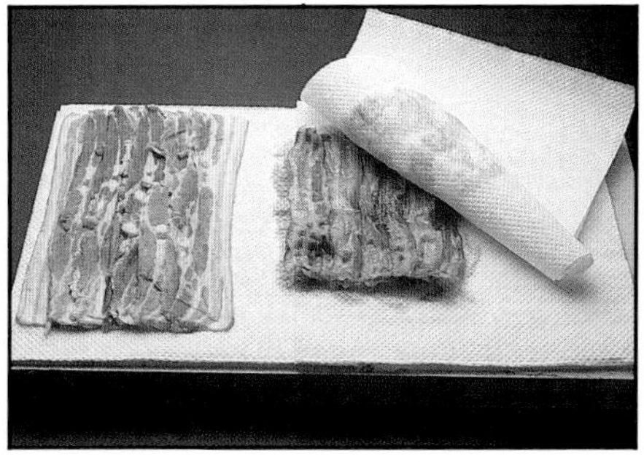

Paper towels are ideal for wrapping fatty foods such as bacon. They absorb the grease during the cooking process.

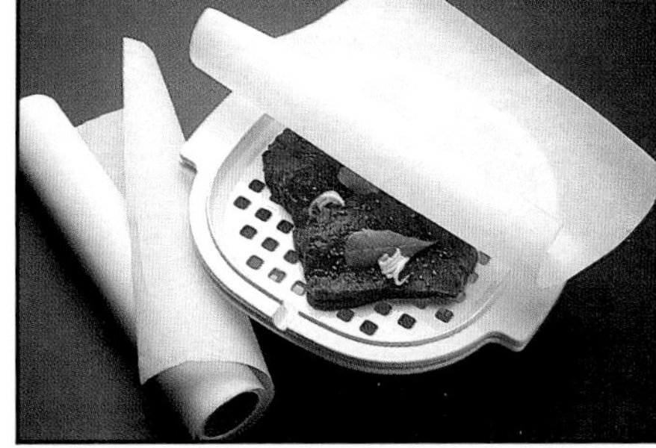

Wax paper is generally used to cover meat and fowl, and as a rule, any slightly fatty foods; you can also use it to wrap food that is to be steamed.

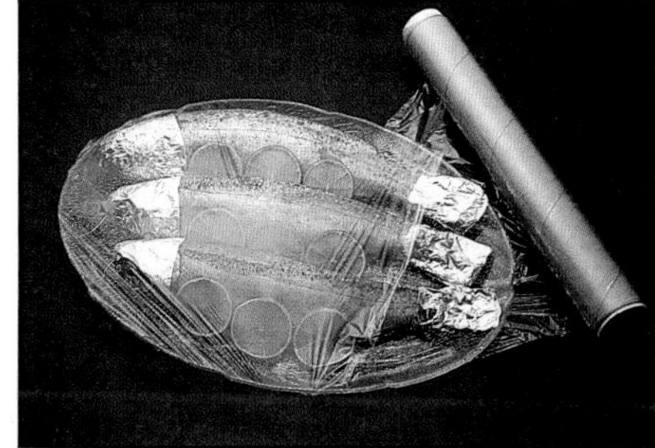

Plastic wrap and plastic cooking pouches can be used to cover most dishes, especially fish and lean foods. Be sure to pierce a hole in the covering to allow the steam to escape.

What care must be taken when removing the Plastic Wrap from foods cooked in the microwave?

Even though the container may not be hot to the touch after the cooking process, the steam contained under the plastic cover is extremely hot. Be very careful when removing the covering. It is important to protect both hands and eyes from contact with this excess heat. The best method is to uncover a small opening and wait a few minutes before removing all the plastic wrapping.

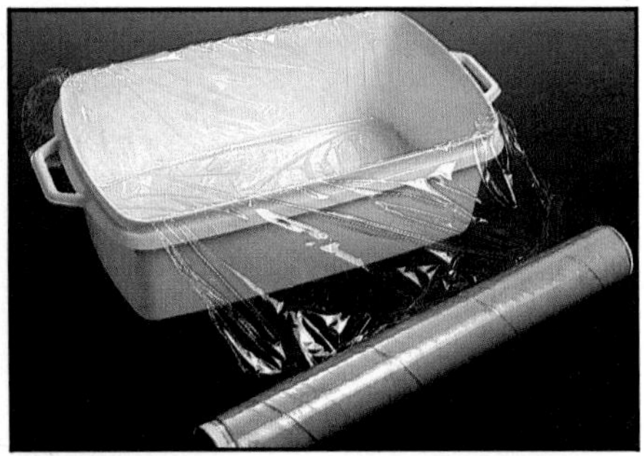

Plastic wrap is also handy for lining dishes containing pâté, terrine, meat loaves and even cakes. To line the pan, simply spread the plastic along the width of the pan...

... then apply another sheet of plastic along the length of the dish. Remove all air pockets before pouring in the prepared food. When the pâté, the terrine, the meat loaf or cake is cooked, remove by pulling the four corners of the plastic wrap from the bottom of the dish. Then lightly pull the wrap away from the food itself.

What are the advantages of lining molds with Plastic Wrap?

Not only will your cake or pie unmold more easily, you no longer need to grease or oil the bottom and sides of any mold, tin or pan. Cooking this way is lighter and healthier.

Use this procedure only with specially designed microwave dishes. Ordinary cookwave may heat to a high enough temperature to melt the plastic wrap.

Aluminum Foil

As we explained on page 14, aluminum foil is forbidden in microwave cooking, with certain exceptions.

The problem with aluminum foil when used in large quantities is that it reflects waves; in other words, it inhibits the cooking process.

However, that fault can become an advantage when small cooking surfaces are covered with aluminum foil in order to delay the cooking process of some portions of food. In such cases, microwave cooking with aluminum foil is not dangerous.

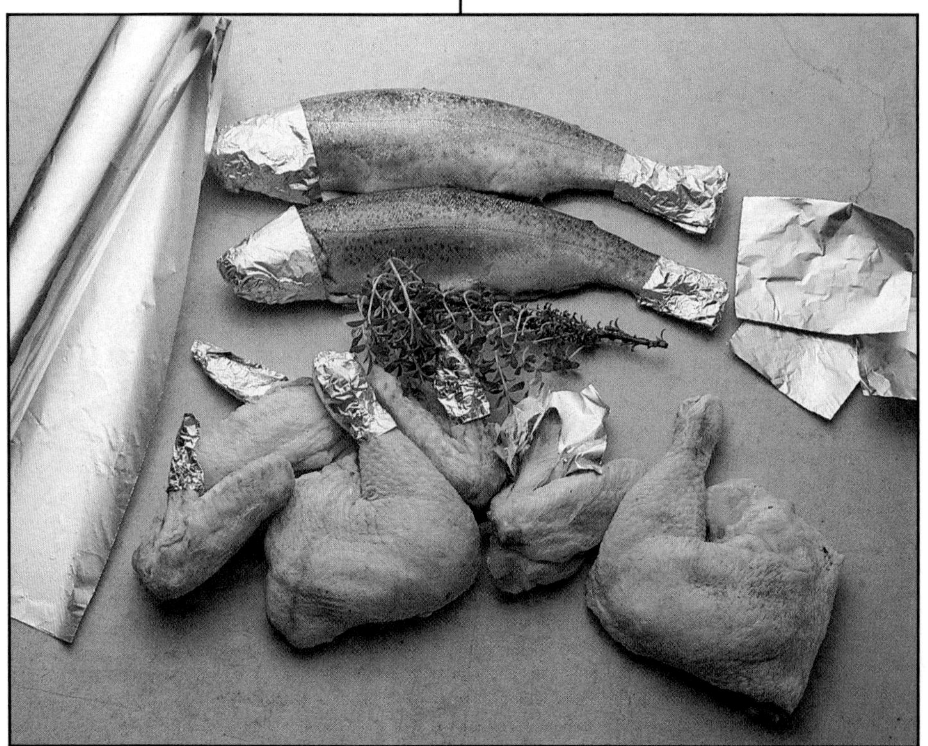

Aluminum foil is useful for protecting delicate ingredients: fish heads or tails, chicken wing tips and drumsticks, the ends of a roast, the ends of bones on chops, etc. The foil is usually removed midway through the cooking process to ensure that the covered parts are cooked.

Advice, Tricks and Secrets

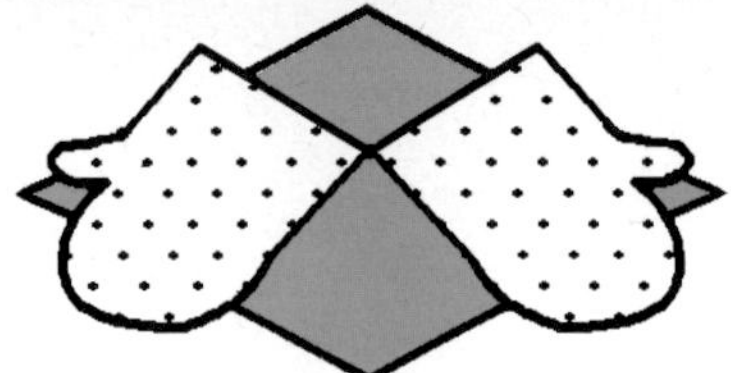

Defrosting

Frozen foods and fresh foods need different treatment. Prior to cooking, frozen food must be defrosted and it is important to follow certain rules.

What Are the Basic Rules for Defrosting?

There are 10 simple rules for defrosting properly:

1. Use the defrost cycle, if there is one on the oven. Otherwise, set the oven at LOW, power level 3 or 30% power.
2. Set the thawing time precisely. (Consult the chart below).
3. Defrost the food in two stages; the first stage being twice as long as the second. (Consult the chart below).
4. Let the food stand after each stage (See chart below).
5. Leave the food to be thawed in its original wrapping during the first stage unless the wrapping contains metal.
6. Unwrap the food at the end of the first stage and set it in an appropriate container.
7. Midway through defrosting, turn the food if it comes in one piece (such as a roast) or stir it lightly (sauce, rice, peas, shrimp, ground meat, etc.)
8. To protect delicate parts of the food from cooking before the rest is thawed, cover them with aluminum foil as described earlier.
9. Half way through defrosting, insert a thermometer into the centre of the food to gauge the process more accurately.
10. At the first sign that the food is cooking, remove it from the oven even though the thawing process may not be complete. Finish defrosting at room temperature.

Defrosting Chart for common foods

FOOD	WEIGHT
Beef (roast)	2 lbs (900 g)
Beef (steak)	7 oz (200 g)
Beef (ground)	18 oz (500 g)
Bread	14 oz (400 g)
Butter	9 oz (250 g)
Chicken (whole)	2 lbs (900 g)
Chicken (pieces)	2 lbs (900 g
Chops (lamb, etc.)	18 oz (500 g)
Duck	2 lbs(900 g)
Fish (whole)	18 oz (500 g)
Fish (filet)	18 oz (500 g)
Fruit	18 oz (500 g)
Pies, Fruit	9 oz (250 g
Pizza	9 oz (250 g)
Pork (roast)	2 lbs (900 g)
Pork (ribs)	18 oz (500 g)
Puddings	9 oz (250 g
Rice, cooked	9 oz (250 g)
Sausages	18 oz (500 g)
Shrimp and oysters	9 oz (250 g)
Stew	2 lbs (900 g)
Turkey	4½ lbs (2 kg
Vegetables	2 lbs (900 g)

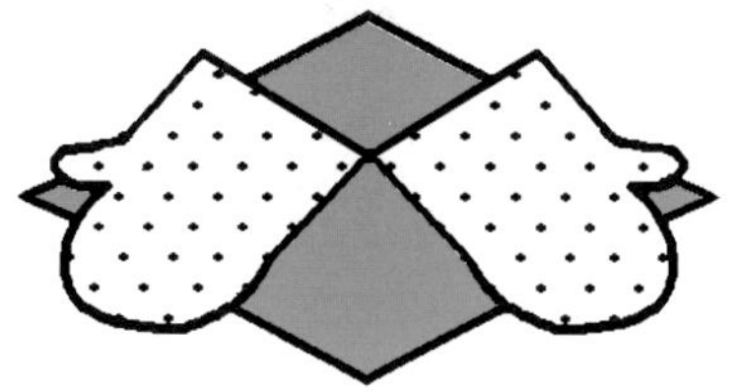

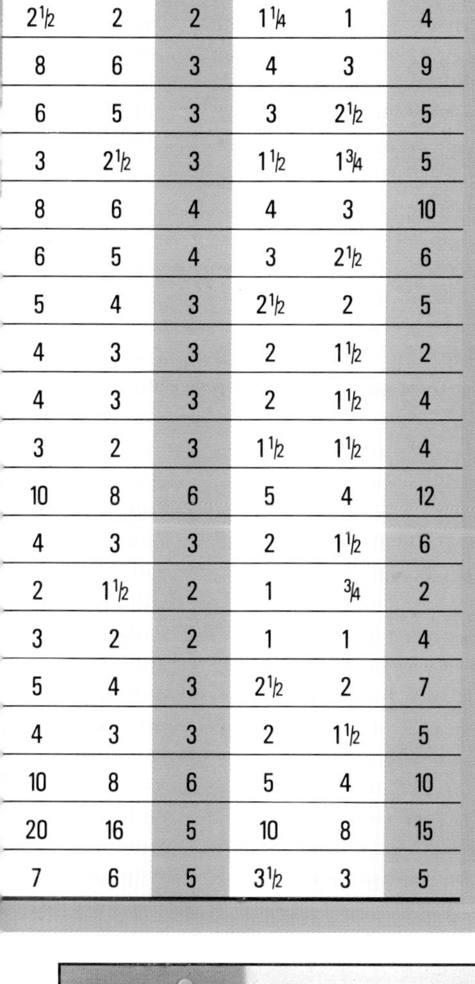

STAGE 1 (min)		STANDING 1	STAGE 2 (min)		STANDING 2
500/650W.	700W.		500/650W.	700W.	
7	6	3	3½	3	10
2	1½	3	1	¾	5
3	2½	3	2	1½	5
4	3	4	2	1½	6
2½	2	2	1¼	1	4
8	6	3	4	3	9
6	5	3	3	2½	5
3	2½	3	1½	1¾	5
8	6	4	4	3	10
6	5	4	3	2½	6
5	4	3	2½	2	5
4	3	3	2	1½	2
4	3	3	2	1½	4
3	2	3	1½	1½	4
10	8	6	5	4	12
4	3	3	2	1½	6
2	1½	2	1	¾	2
3	2	2	1	1	4
5	4	3	2½	2	7
4	3	3	2	1½	5
10	8	6	5	4	10
20	16	5	10	8	15
7	6	5	3½	3	5

Tips and techniques for even cooking

Once again, it is important to remember that the cooking process in a microwave oven is not the same as in a conventional oven.

The waves reach the outer layers of food first, and spread slowly toward the center, so that food in the center of the container cooks more gradually.

What are the Rules for Even Cooking?

Simply follow the following guidelines:

Circular Arrangement of Food

Because the cooking process starts at the periphery of the dish, it is best to arrange food in a circular fashion.

Larger Pieces Towards the Edge of the Cooking Dish

Arrange the larger pieces towards the outside of the cooking dish where they will cook faster, and the smaller pieces towards the center.

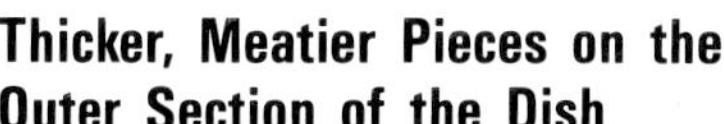

Thicker, Meatier Pieces on the Outer Section of the Dish

For the same reason always arrange the meatier, thicker pieces of fowl or meats on the perimeter of the dish; the lean or bony sections towards the middle.

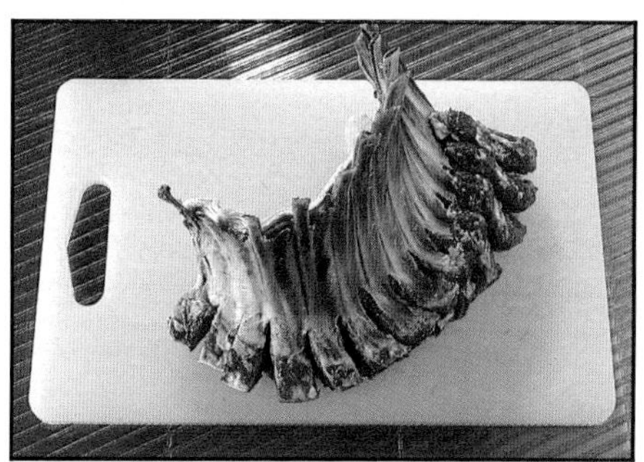

A crown roast of lamb cooks more evenly than a rack of lamb.

The filet portion of meats (the most tender part) cooks more quickly than the lean meat around the bones; but because the filet part is thicker, cooking will be even. Use small pieces of aluminum foil to prevent the bones from charring.

The Use of the Shelf

As in any conventional oven, the shelf serves a dual purpose: it provides a second cooking area, and makes it possible to bring the food closer to the energy source if it is in the roof of the oven (as is the case with most microwave ovens and with regular ovens on broiler position).

Is it Possible to Cook Food on the Hearth and the Shelf at the Same Time?
Yes, it is. But you will have to follow a few rules or use two or three "tricks".

Theoretically, when cooking food on the hearth and the shelf at the same time, the food on the hearth should require longer cooking. However, it is actually possible to plan identical cooking times — an important factor when planning a meal — by cleverly distributing the food in the oven space.

When cooking the same recipe on two levels, set twice as much on top as on the bottom. The six tomatoes on the top will take about the same time to cook as the three on the bottom.

To ensure the equal distribution of waves. Arrange food so that items on the shelf do not block food on the bottom.

When cooking pizzas, pies or other foods which might boil over or drip, spread wax paper on the shelf to protect the food cooking on the lower shelf.

When cooking identical foods, another suggestion is to put exactly the same quantity in both dishes and switch their positions in the oven midway through cooking. To avoid confusion, identify each dish with a small piece of vegetable.

Is it Possible to Cook a Meat Dish and a Vegetable Dish at the Same Time?
It is unrealistic to try to cook a meat dish and a vegetable dish for the same length of time, but you can certainly cook them both in the same time period.

All you need is a little experience and some familiarity with your particular oven.

When cooking this roast turkey in the top of the oven and its accompanying dish of green peas on the bottom shelf, cooking time is easily balanced. If the peas are done before the meat, simply slip the pea dish directly under the roast; the cooking process is greatly reduced but the dish remains warm. The same technique applies if the roast is done before the vegetables.

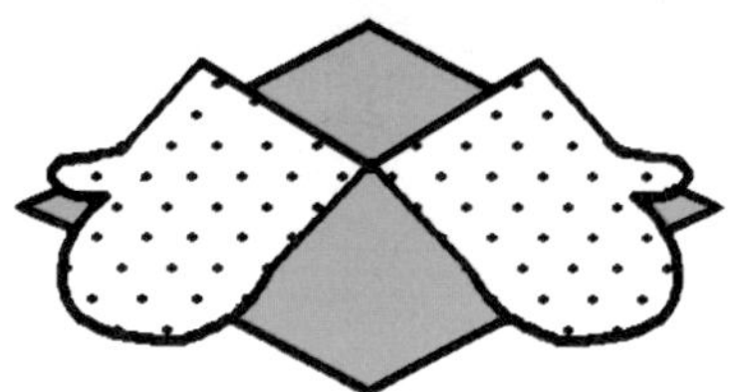

Quantities and cooking time

Cooking is an exact science, but 1 and 1 do not always make 2!

For example, in a conventional oven, a piece of meat weighing 2 lbs (900 g) is ready in 30 minutes, but a 4 lb (1.8 kg) piece cooks in 45 minutes rather than 60. In this case: 1 + 1 = 1.5!

Conversely, in a microwave oven, although a piece of meat weighing 1 lb is ready in 6 minutes, a 2 lb (1.8 kg) piece will not take 12 minutes but 15 minutes to cook. In this case: 1 + 1 = 2.5!

Is there a saving of time and energy if large quantities are cooked in two batches?
Quite often, yes, especially when dealing with foods that need quick cooking. Cooking in two smaller batches gives more even cooking, is easier to monitor, and saves both time and energy.

When preparing a dish in two batches, is there not a risk that the first batch will turn cold while the second is cooking?
Not at all. Often, the cooking time for each batch is very short. Also note that the temperature continues to rise in foods taken out of the microwave oven during the standing time (see page 38). It does not cool as quickly as one might think.

Cooking peas in four ramekins set two at a time in the microwave takes half the time it would to cook all four portions in one large ramekin. It also eliminates the bother of frequent stirring, with the risk of crushing the peas in the process.

It takes 3 minutes to warm up a 1 lb (450 g) vegetable medley in a small dish. Twice that amount in a larger dish takes 9 minutes. It is possible to cook 3 lbs (1.3 kg) in three batches in about the same time as it takes to cook 2 lbs (900 g) in a single batch. Also, cooking is more even in a smaller dish. You can even begin serving the first batch while the second is still cooking. You will have hot vegetables throughout the entire meal.

As a general rule, remember that a microwave oven is not a food storage bin! If it is overly "fed", it loses most of its advantages, just as a refrigerator loses its ability to keep food cold if packed too full.

Three Interesting Examples of Time-Saving

3 potatoes
8 min. cooking time

3 potatoes
8 min. cooking time = 16 min.

6 potatoes
20 min. cooking time

Time saved: 4 minutes

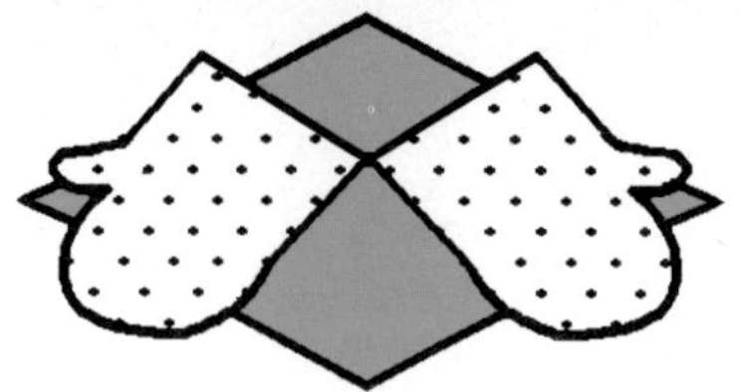

Stirring, an Indispensable Move

We know that foods in a microwave oven do not cook evenly; the heating process begins on the perimeter.

This makes it essential to redistribute the ingredients of a particular dish.

There is only way to do it. Stir.

Stirring is an unpleasant task when working with a conventional oven because of the intense heat and the risk of burns. But with a microwave oven, it is as easy as child's play. The steps are simple to follow: Open the microwave oven door (automatically, the magnetron stops functioning), stir the ingredients with a wooden spoon, close the door and readjust the cooking program. The entire operation should take no more than 10 seconds!

What is the Best Way to Stir Food?
That depends on the recipe.

The term ''stir'' applies mainly to foods such as sauces, creams, soups and purees, or to more or less liquid foods like rice, peas, or dishes containing chopped or minced food. (For details about larger ingredients, consult page 28).

In the Case of a Liquid Foods

It is easy to see that the cooking process is faster around the edges.

Using a wooden spoon, move the ingredients from the edges towards the center and vice-versa.

This move ensures even cooking.

In the Case of a Dish Containing Small Pieces of Solid Food

The stirring method is the same as with liquid foods, from the outside towards the center but, in this case, also by moving the pieces at the bottom of the dish to the surface. For vegetables, as illustrated here, stir gently so as not to crush them.

How often Should Foods be Stirred?
That depends mainly on the cooking time and the type of ingredients. The following chart gives a fairly accurate indication:

COOKING TIME	NUMBER OF STIRS	
	DELICATE INGREDIENTS sauces, etc.	OTHER INGREDIENTS soups, vegetables, etc.
Less than 5 min	3 times	2 times
From 5 to 10 min	5 times	3 times
More than 10 min	5 times	3 times
	+ 2 times every 5 min over 10 min	+ once every 5 min after 10 min

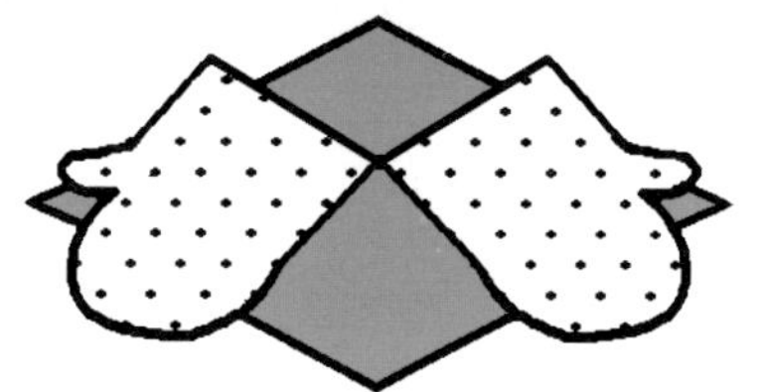

Power Levels for Delicate Sauces

We stated on page 13 that most cooking is done at HIGH, or maximum power, which is setting 10 on most microwave ovens.

There are exceptions to this rule, however. In the chapter on meats, we will see why certain cuts of meat require a longer cooking period at lower power.

Fine sauces with a cream, butter or egg base should be cooked at MEDIUM, or half the capacity of the microwave oven. This corresponds to setting or power level 5.

Here are two spoonfuls of a same sauce. The spoonful on the left was cooked on HIGH; it separated. The spoonful on the right, cooked on MEDIUM, remained homogenous.

This is because fats are more susceptible to waves than other foods: if cooked too quickly, they separate from the other elements and the sauce curdles.

Is a Sauce Spoiled if it Curdles or Separates?

Normally, it is possible to repair the damage by adding a spoonful of lukewarm water to the mix and running the sauce through a blender. Once the sauce has returned to its original homogenous texture, it should not be reheated but served immediately.

Covering Fatty Foods

Foods with a high fat content such as meatballs, sausage or duck, should be covered during cooking.
If molecules of fat are over-exposed to microwaves, they tend to cook too much and the food becomes dry and hard.

Add a spoonful of lukewarm water. Pour the entire mixture into another container through a fine sieve.

Stir the separated sauce with a whisk to force it through the sieve; it will return to its original texture.

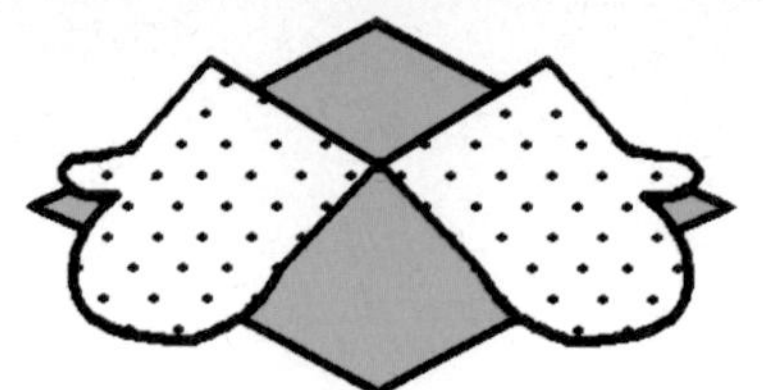

Turning Food During the Cooking Process

For the same reason that we stir liquids or semi-liquids to obtain even cooking throughout the dish, larger pieces of food must be turned during the cooking process.

Ideally, steak and meat slices should be turned at least three times during the cooking process so that each side is exposed at least twice to the microwaves.

Pieces of meat cooked in a sauce should be turned at least once during the cooking process, and if possible, two or three times.

Baked potatoes only need to be turned once, midway through the cooking process, but will be smoother if they are turned at least three times!

Skewered cubes of meat should be rotated a quarter turn at least three times during the cooking process so that all four sides of the meat are equally exposed to the microwaves.

Doesn't the Constant Opening and Closing of the Microwave Oven Door to Stir or Turn Food Affect Cooking Time?

In theory, a microwave oven does not react in the same way as a conventional oven when the door is opened.

Since the air in the oven is not heated, it doesn't lose heat when the door is open, so if the oven door is opened for a few seconds, the cooking process is not interrupted.

In practice though, we noticed that three or four regular interruptions, however brief, affected the total cooking time of a dish.

Therefore, its a good idea to compensate for the amount of time during which cooking is interrupted by adding to the total cook time. Calculate as follows:

1 pause : negligeable
2 pauses: add 20 seconds
3 pauses: add 30 seconds
4 pauses: add 40 seconds
5 pauses: add 1 minutes
6 pauses: add 1 1/4 minutes
7 pauses: add 1 1/2 minutes
8 pauses: add 2 minutes

How Serious Is It if the Food Is Not Cooked at the End of Cooking?

Not serious at all. It might be a catastrophe if the food is overcooked because it is impossible to "uncook" it, but you can certainly recook a dish.

However it is best to cook foods as accurately as possible, especially when one is a novice at microwave cooking. You will learn to adjust cooking times to your own taste without ever spoiling a recipe.

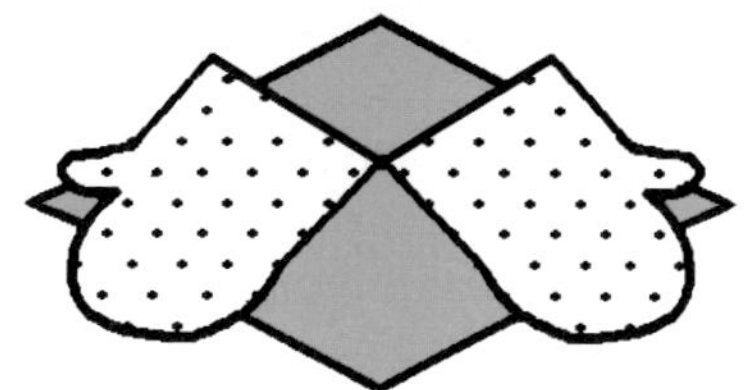

Turning Dishes

As we have seen, stirring or turning foods in the microwave produces a more evenly cooked dish.

The absence of heat inside the microwave oven has certain advantages; but a few disadvantages. Food is not "bathed" in the heat as in a conventional oven. It cooks where the waves penetrate first; the interior is cooked by heat diffusion.

Since it is important to obtain even cooking, the dish should be turned in order to expose every angle and corner to microwave action.

This is the procedure:

First position of the dish in the oven: The spoon is at the top left; the dish is vertical.

Second position of the dish in the oven: The spoon is at the top right; the dish is in a horizontal position.

Third position of the dish in the oven: The spoon is at the bottom right; the dish is again in a vertical position.

Continue to turn the dish a quarter turn every three minutes.

The Microwave Turntable

The tedious task of turning a dish at regular intervals during the cooking process can be done automatically. Actually, some microwave ovens are equipped with a turntable that turns continuously throughout the cooking process.

However, if your oven does not have this feature, you can buy a spring loaded turntable. You simply wind it up for a full hour of continous, regular turning.

A simple tray equipped with a spring...

and the dish cooks evenly, while turning.

Does the Turntable Limit the Usable Space in the Oven?

Admittedly, the principle of the turntable does not apply very well to rectangular or long dishes. They tend to bump into the walls and do occasionally get stuck.

Round cookware, preferably without handles, is the best choice when using a turntable.

Test your cookware on the turntable before cooking in it. If the cookware touches the sides, even slightly, opt for smaller dishes or simply don't use the turntable.

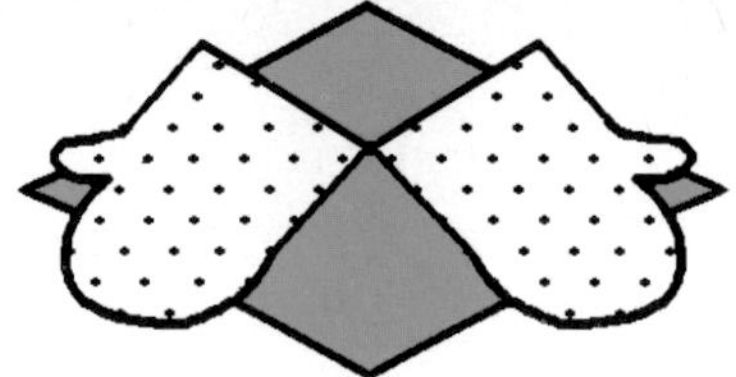

Browning and Roasting Mixes

Browning plates and dishes are most practical for frying food, (meat in particular), to give it a lovely golden appearance.

To brown meat without a browning plate, you should probably use one of the commercially prepared products. There is a large selection of high quality, including "Bouquet" and "B.B.Q." sauce.

However, it is often more interesting and gratifying to prepare one's own mixture, and adapt it to taste for different meats.

A browning or roasting mix generally contains two elements: a binding agent, often of a syrup-like texture, and a coloring agent, which intensifies caramelization and gives food its golden color.

Honey, maple syrup, corn syrup, table syrup, caramel and molasses are common browning agents. Paprika and soya sauce are often added because they enhance browning without altering taste.

To prepare this browning mix, simply combine three parts syrup, two parts soya sauce and one part paprika.

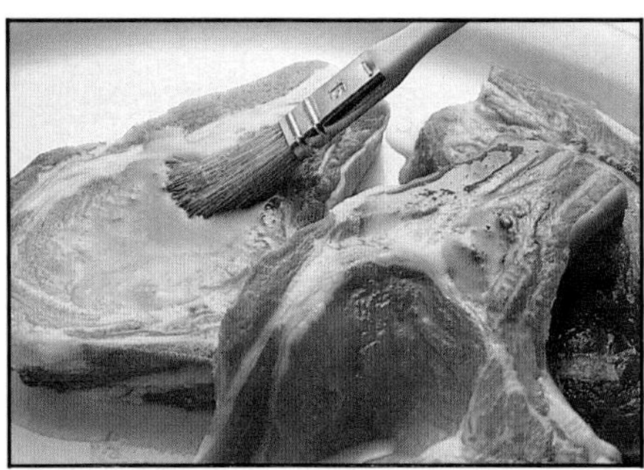

With a kitchen brush, spread the mixture on all sides of the meat. Repeat the procedure during the cooking process.

It produces a lovely golden color that sharpens the appetite without altering the taste of the meat. At worst, a "picky" eater may detect a slight, yet quite tasty, sweet and sour flavor. For those who will not tolerate any sweet taste, the syrup agent may be replaced with butter, combined with the soya sauce and paprika. Caution: Do not add salt, the soya sauce contains a fair amount.

Is there any difference in appearance between food cooked as is and food coated with a browning mixture?

The pictures on the next page say it all!

The same duck has been cut in two.

The half on the left was cooked in the microwave oven "au naturel" while the one on the right was cooked in a coating of a mixture made up of the following ingredients:

6 parts maple syrup
2 parts soya sauce
1 part paprika

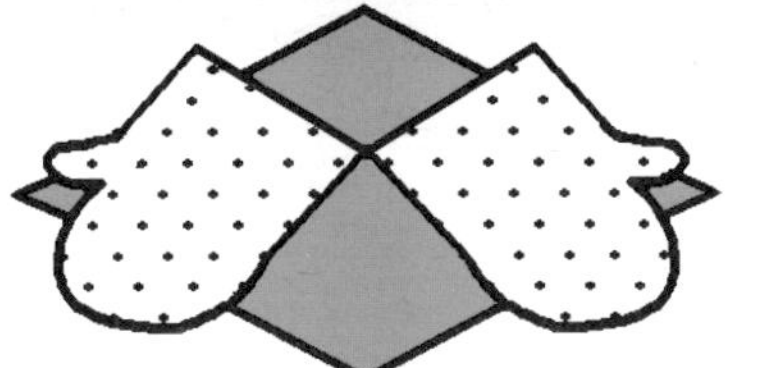

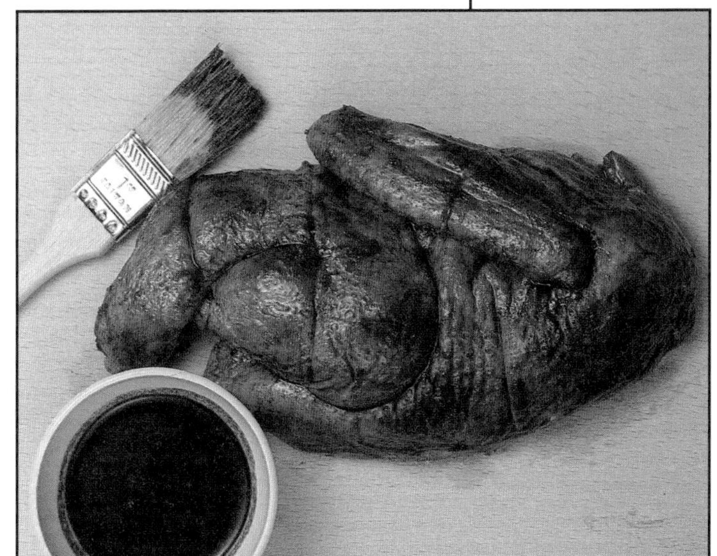

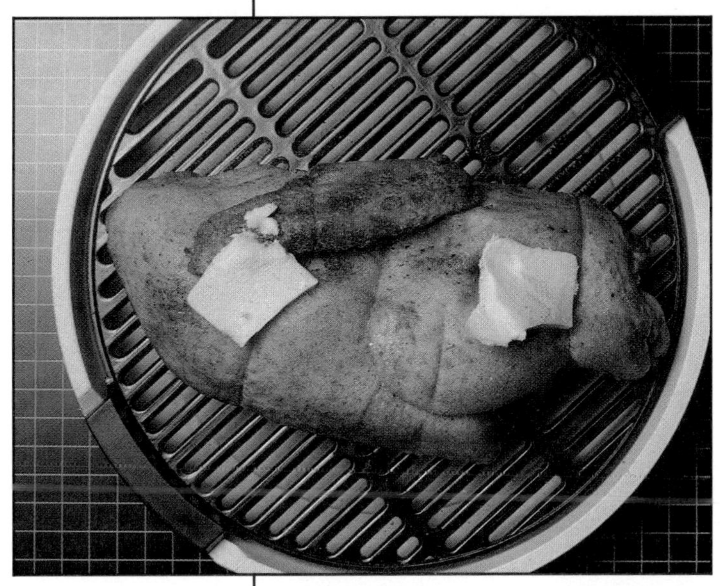

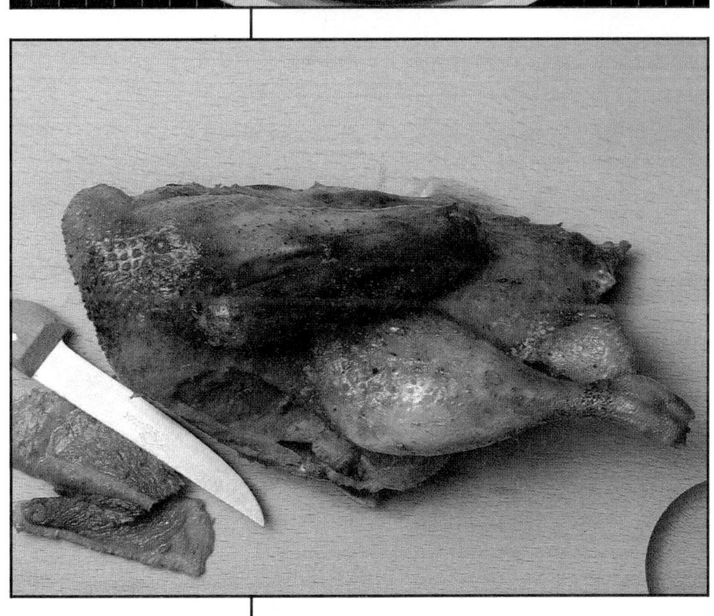

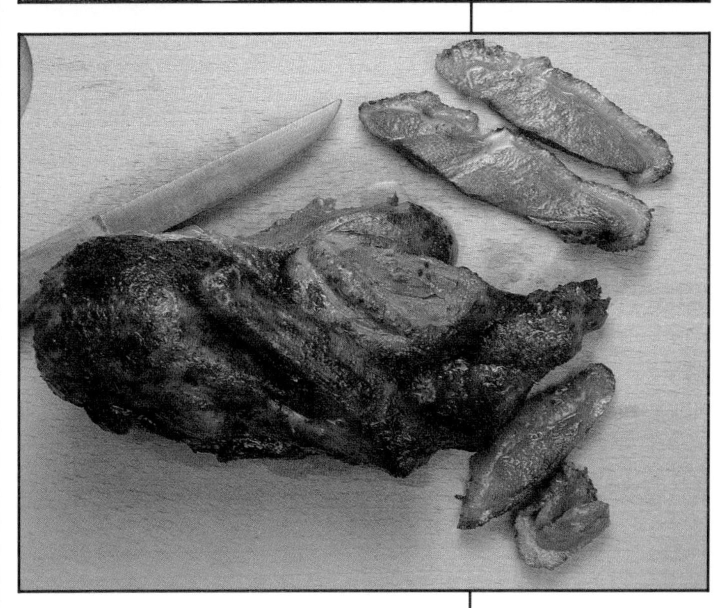

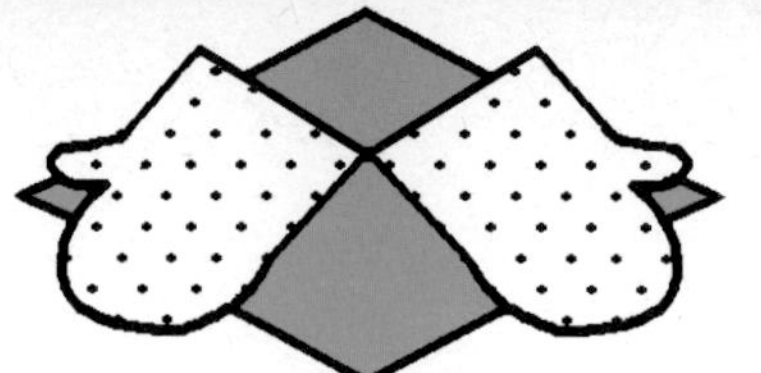

Glazing

Glazing is a technique which consists of coating food with specific ingredients that enhance flavor and give a glossy appearance and a look of freshness.

There are two types of glazes. Glazes for sweets and desserts, usually with a melted chocolate base or a fruit jelly base, will be discussed at length in the chapter on desserts. A ''salty'' glaze is used to coat main dishes, particularly poultry and meat. It is interesting to note that the so-called ''salty'' glazes rarely are... They have acquired their name from the foods that they coat, which usually contain salt.

''Salty'' glazes usually contain one ingredient which sticks to the food (fruit jelly, sugar or gelatin), another ingredient for aroma, giving flavor to the mixture (fruit juices, tomato juice, liqueurs, vinegar, soya sauce, Worcestershire sauce), and finally a touch of herbs and spices. Dessert glazes usually have a chocolate, fruit jelly, gelatin or egg base.

For example, combine six parts currant jelly, two parts wine vinegar and a good pinch of powdered ginger.

Run through the microwave oven for 1 minute at HIGH to liquify the mixture, and keep it warm.

Using a brush, coat a piece of poultry or meat. At the end of the cooking process this piece of turkey will have a lovely glazed, crispy texture. Repeat the coating process as often as desired.

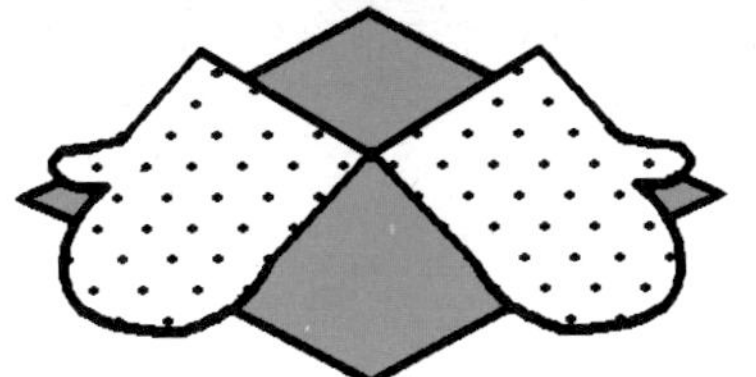

Gelatin

Certain recipes in this book call for gelatine. It is important to learn how to use it.

Gelatin, in either powder or sheet form, must always be dissolved before use. Simply put the required amount of gelatin in a bowl with a small amount of lukewarm water. When it begins to dissolve or soften, set it in the microwave oven at HIGH for 30 seconds. The gelatin will be completely liquified.

Blend the dissolved gelatin into the mixture and allow it to set in the refrigerator for at least 2 hours.

Depending on the manufacturer, gelatin may come in either powder or sheet form.
1 sheet = 1 tbsp of powdered gelatin and they are equally good.

Gratins

Cooking a dish au gratin involves topping the food with grated cheese before putting it in the oven.

In a conventional oven, the cheese melts and turns golden brown and crispy, giving the food a lovely "gratin" appearance. In the microwave oven, however, even though the cheese may melt more rapidly, it does not take on the same attractive golden brown appearance we find in dishes cooked the conventional way.

There are a few "tricks" to circumvent this problem. The first option is to run the dish under a regular broiler just prior to serving. But it is annoying to have to use two appliances for one dish, especially since the broiler of a conventional oven needs preheating.

So here is an easy way to produce equally satisfying results.

Since microwave cooking does not produce the desired golden brown tint, you have to provide the color first. Simply use ingredients that are already colored.

Certain types of cheese, such as Edam and some cheddars, have a lovely yellow, orange or even a coral color. When grated over food, their natural color will enhance the appearance of a dish.

White cheeses, such as gruyère or parmesan, make very attractive gratin dishes when sprinkled with brightly colored spices such as paprika, saffron or curry powder.

These small gratinée canapés, cooked in the microwave oven for a few seconds, are very pleasing to the eye.

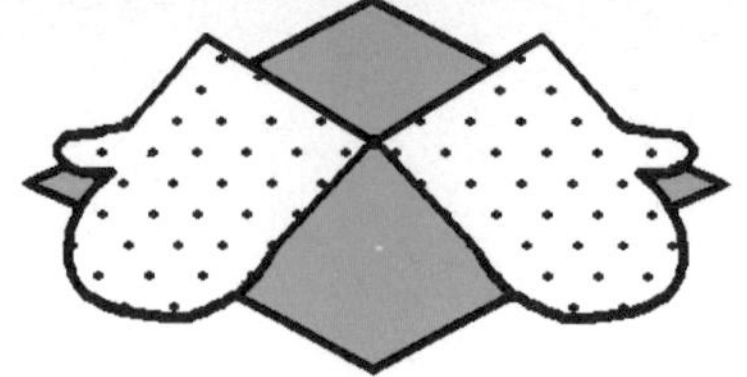

Blanching Vegetables

The microwave oven is well-known for its ability to defrost foods, but it is equally useful in the preparation of foods for home-freezing.

When vegetables are in season and can be bought for a modest price, why not stock up and prepare them for winter meals? The microwave oven is a perfect tool for blanching vegetables.

What Does "Blanching" Mean?
The term simply means precooking the food for a short time at boiling temperature. This process helps to retain the maximum flavor of the food. Blanching food is a very simple process with a microwave oven. Proceed as follows:

Choose, for instance, some good fresh zucchini. Wash and slice them.

Put them in a dish. Add one cup of water but no salt.

Why Should You Avoid Salting Vegetables Before Cooking?
Athough cooking water may be salted, the vegetables themselves should not be salted because salt tends to burn in a microwave oven and might darken the vegetables. It is always best to salt at the end of cooking.

Set in the oven at HIGH until the water begins to boil. (The time that it takes the water to boil depends on the amount of zucchini in the dish.)

Cover the dish and let stand for 3 minutes.

Stop the cooking process by immersing the zucchini in ice cold water.

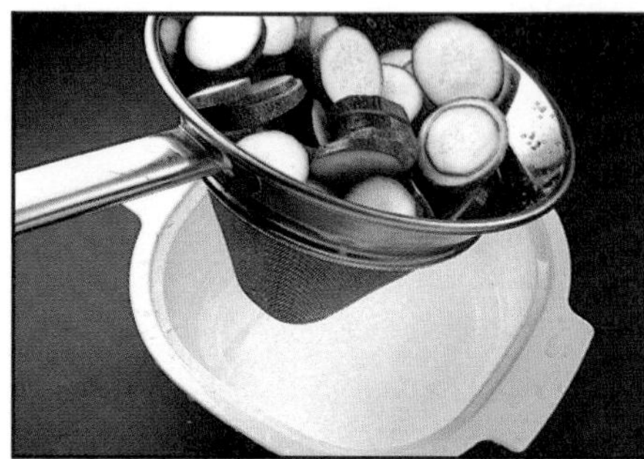

Carefully drain the zucchini.

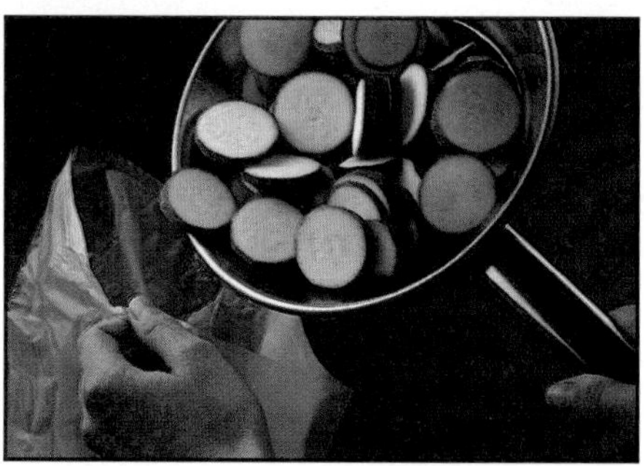

Put the vegetables in a freezer bag.

Close and tag the bag, mark the date and freeze.

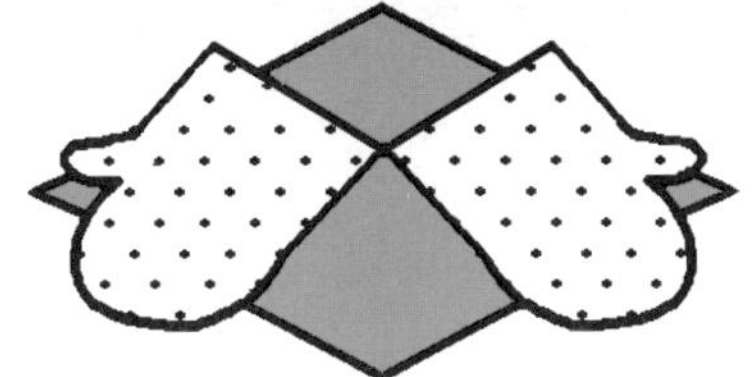

Everyday Cooking

Can You Cook Pasta in the Microwave Oven?

Many people think that pasta cooked in the microwave oven will just dry up. But with the right procedure, you can actually make delicious pasta in the microwave.

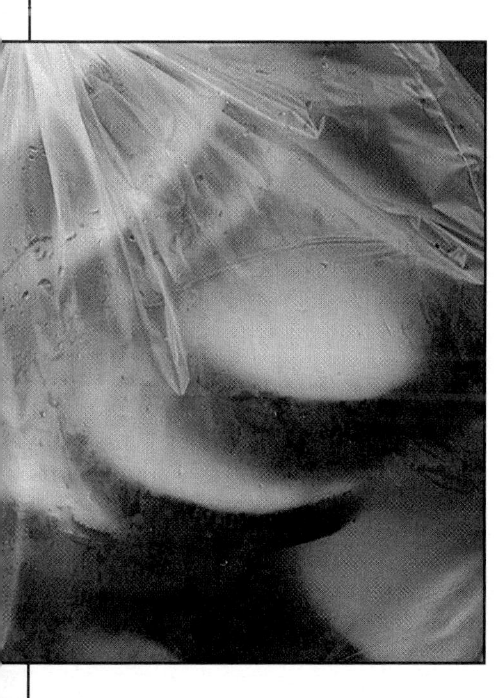

The best way to cook pasta in the microwave is to steam it. For instance, set a required amount of tagliatelli in a steamer basket, and one cup of salted water in the bottom container.

Place the basket over the dish. Cover both and cook on HIGH.

In just a few minutes, you will have tender, appetizing tagliatelli, all ready to serve. Vary cooking times according to the type of microwave oven, the type of pasta (fresh, dehydrated or frozen), and the amount required; (refer to the vegetable cooking chart on page 197.)

What is the Best Way to Toast Bread?

Toasting bread in a microwave oven is just as tricky as preparing a gratin dish (see page 35). Bread will come out toasted, but without its normal brown coloring.

If you have no toaster, it is practically impossible to make the crispy, golden toast that is standard fare.

However, if you like bread lightly toasted, you will appreciate the speed and neatness of making toast in your microwave.

Spread the bread slices lightly with salted butter.

Set the bread on the microwave cooking shelf. Set the oven at HIGH and cook for 2 or 3 minutes, to taste.

This produces tender, pale golden toast, ready to eat or to be used in other recipes.

Dehydrating Fresh Herbs

The season for fresh herbs is extremely short, and the rest of the year they are impossible to find or very expensive.

The microwave oven is ideal for dehydrating herbs and seasonings. The procedure is quite simple:

In season, purchase all the fresh herbs you will need for the year.

Set each variety of herbs between two sheets of paper towel and set in the microwave oven for 5 minutes at HIGH.

Crush them with your fingers.

Store them in tightly sealed jars to retain their aroma and flavor. Do not forget to label the jars, for when dried, herbs look alike.

Are Fresh Herbs and Dried Herbs Used in the Same Proportions?
Absolutely not. Unfortunately, many cookbooks do not specify which to use.

Once herbs have been dried, they have less flavor than when fresh. Dehydration, however, tends to increase their aromatic qualities.

What Type of Herbs are Used in the Recipes in This Book?
Fresh herbs, naturally! A chef would never think of using anything else. But we recognize that dried herbs, when properly dehydrated under the best conditions, as described above, can come in quite handy on those "rainy days".

When a recipe calls for 1 tablespoon of fresh herbs, you can substitute 1 teaspoon of the same herb in dehydrated form.

Remember, 1 teaspoon of dehydrated herbs is equal to 1 tablespoon of fresh herbs.

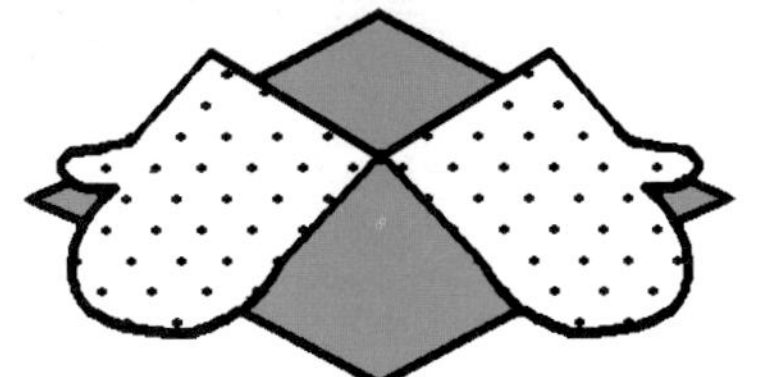

Potatoes and Eggs

Certain foods particularly benefit from microwave cooking.

One example is baked potatoes, which become softer and taste better than those cooked by any other method, and in a third of the time.

The same is true for eggs, whether fried, scrambled or in an omelet. They cook in a flash and come out especially light.

Eggs and potatoes require a little preparation before cooking...

Pierce the egg yolk very delicately with a toothpick.

Prick potato skins with a fork. If you omit this procedure the egg or potato will eventually expand and crack.

Why Should You Never Cook an Egg in Its Shell in the Microwave Oven?

We asked ourselves the same question, and although we had an idea what would happen, we decided to put it to the test. See for yourselves:

We put an egg in the oven, set at HIGH.

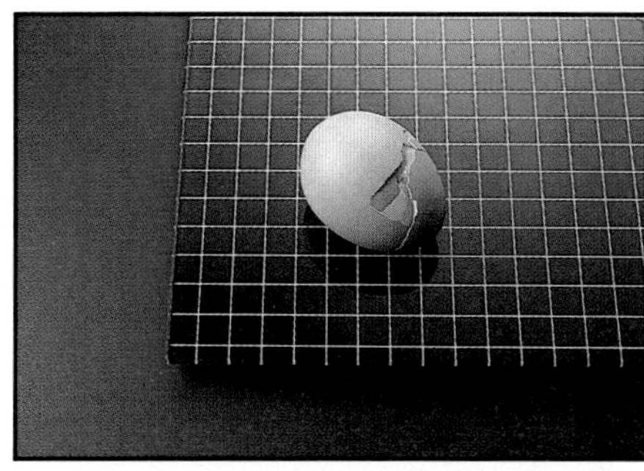

After a few seconds, it began to crack.

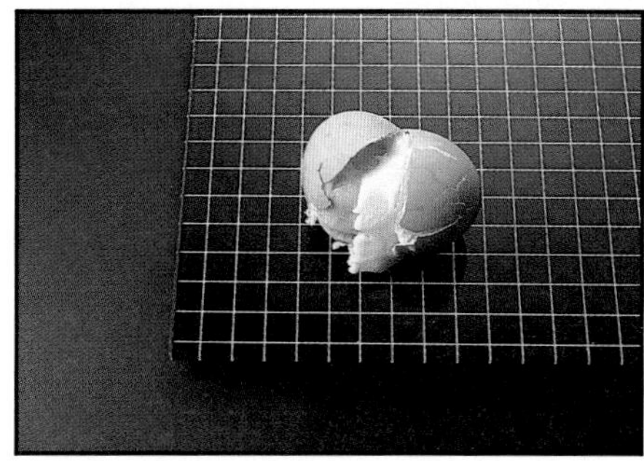

After 1 minute, it shattered...

And after 2 minutes, the egg exploded, covering the oven walls with pulverized egg white and yolk. The cleaning process took nearly 1 hour. It just shows that curiosity is not always rewarded!

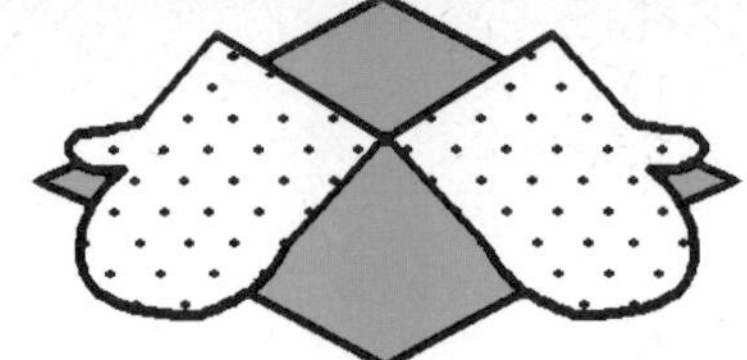

The Temperature Probe

A number of microwave ovens are now equipped with a temperature probe.

This apparatus measures the inner temperature of food during the cooking process.

A thermostat system regulates the cooking time according to pre-set integrated programs. Thus, with the push of a button, you can program how well you want your roast cooked, and the oven does the rest.

The probe is a long flexible cord attached to the inside of the oven, with a long needle which is inserted into the food requiring temperature measurement.

The same thermostatic principle, regulated by a similar mini-computer, is used in other sophisticated devices like the slow cooker, which allows you to simmer a dish at low heat for a long period of time. The slow cooker lets you cook a dish for hours, even while you are away, and automatically keeps food at the right temperature until serving time.

These technical innovations are not a dream but a practical, modern reality. However, these items are not an integral part of every microwave owner's kitchen. Moreover, pre-set programs apply to a limited number of recipes. Other foods must be cooked under the watchful eye of the cook.

We can only repeat our advice on page 13 regarding these "gadgets". Let those who have access to the more sophisticated devices try our methods, and decide for themselves which they prefer.

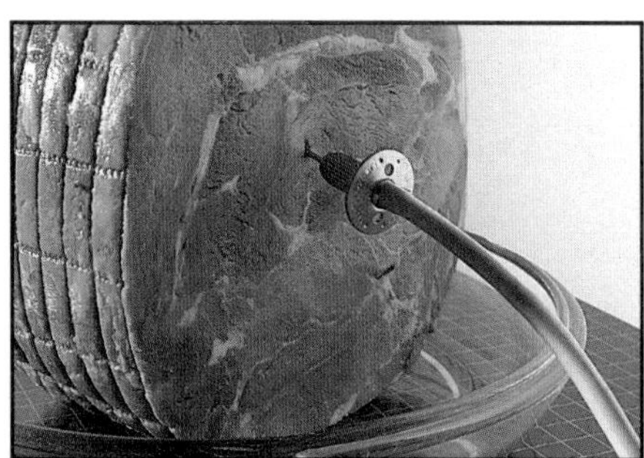

The temperature probe measures the temperature inside the ham.

It regulates power setting and cooking time to achieve the desired stage of doneness.

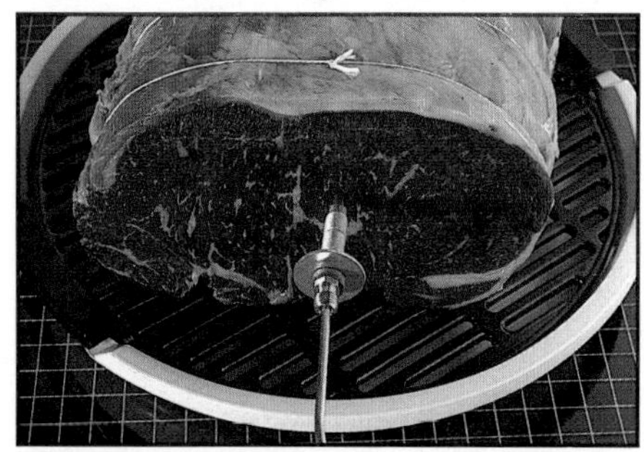

Each probe is manufactured to fit a specific microwave oven. The probe works best when used for large pieces of food.

Standing Time

When the oven stops, the cooking process actually continues for a few minutes. The period of time may vary but it is essential that the standing time be respected.

It is best to cover the dish while it stands. Special lids are available which allow the steam to evaporate.

How Long Should a Dish Be Left to Stand at the End of the Cooking Process?

Allow 3 minutes for dishes cooked less than 5 minutes; 5 minutes for dishes cooked between 5 and 10 minutes. Then add 4 minutes standing time for each additional 10 minute cooking period.

These figures serve only as a guide; we have given precise standing times in each recipe.

About the Presentation of the Recipes

Example:

Number of servings

Power Setting

+ + + HIGH
+ + MEDIUM
+ LOW

Cooking Time for Various Power Levels of Ovens

Standing Time

Calories per serving

Fat Content per serving

Recommended Cookware

122

California Shrimp

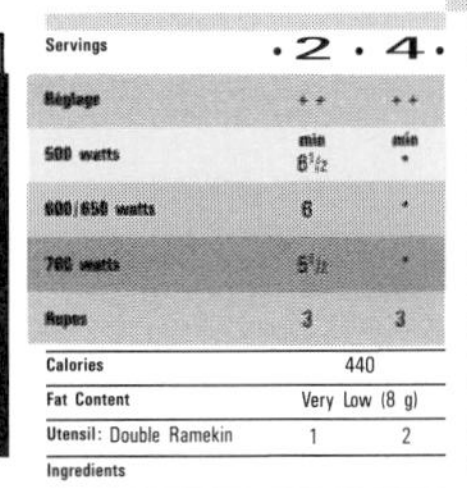

Servings	2	4
Réglage	+ +	+ +
500 watts	min 8 1/2	min *
600/650 watts	6	*
700 watts	5 1/2	*
Repos	3	3
Calories	440	
Fat Content	Very Low (8 g)	
Utensil: Double Ramekin	1	2
Ingredients		
Large peeled shrimp	12 oz (340 g)	1 1/2 lbs (675 g)
Corn niblets	1 cup	2 cups
Small peas	1/2 cup	1 cup
Pineapple slices	2	4
Canned red kidney beans	1/2 cup	1 cup
Red pepper	1/2	1
Orange juice	2 tbsp	4 tbsp
Lemon juice	1 tbsp	2 tbsp
Butter	1 tbsp	2 tbsp
Tabasco sauce	3 drops	6 drops
Salt	1/4 tsp	1/2 tsp

* Cook one dish on top shelf, the other on bottom shelf; exchange position half way through cooking process. Add 2 minutes cooking time.

Carefully drain corn niblets, peas and red kidney beans. Pat shrimp dry. Cut pineapple and green pepper into small pieces.

Distribute ingredients in ramekins.

Add butter, lemon and orange juice mixture, salt and tabasco sauce to ingredients.

- Thoroughly drain corn niblets, peas and kidney beans.
- Pat the shrimp dry with paper towel or cloth.
- Cut the pineapple and red pepper into cubes.
- Arrange corn niblets in bottom of ramekins. Add shrimp, red pepper, pineapple, peas and kidney beans.
- Blend lemon juice with orange juice, salt and tabasco sauce. Pour over mixture.
- Top with butter. Cover with wax paper.
- Cook in microwave according to chart instructions. Stir twice during cooking process.
- Let stand before serving.

In this recipe the red peppers are still tender-crisp, as in Chinese cooking. If you prefer, precook them with a spoonful of hot water for 3 minutes on HIGH.

Technique

Step-by-step Instructions

Author's Comments

Ingredients of the recipe

– Measurements are given in U.S. Customary system and in metric.

– Abbreviations used are:

tsp	= teaspoon		
tbsp	= tablespoon		
c	= cup	cm	= centimeter
oz	= ounce	l	= liter
lb	= pound	kg	= kilogram
in	= inch	g	= gram
qt	= quart	min	= minute

Amount of herbs are always indicated for fresh herbs. If you use dried herbs use half of the amount indicated.

Entrées

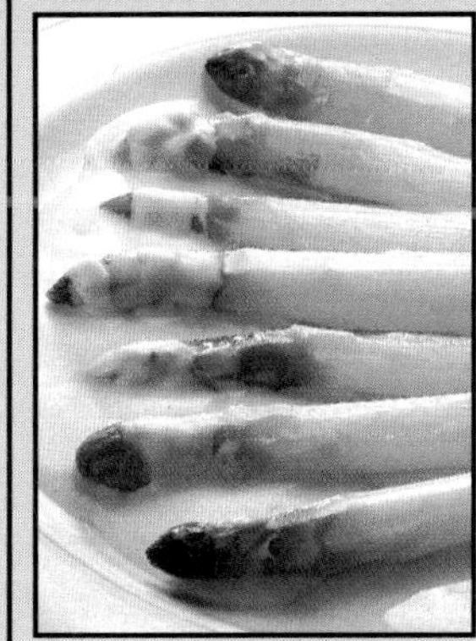

Potatoes stuffed with salmon

Servings	1	2
Setting	+ + +	+ + +
500 watts	min $6^1/_2$	min 10
600/650 watts	$5^1/_2$	9
700 watts	5	$7^1/_2$
Standing time	3	4
Calories	560	
Fat Content	Average (30 g)	
Utensil: Paper towel		
Ingredients		
Potato(es)	1	2
Smoked salmon	1 oz (30 g)	2 oz (60 g)
Butter	1 oz (30 g)	2 oz (60 g)
Whipping cream	1 tbsp	2 tbsp
Lemon or lime juice	1 tsp	2 tsp
Chives (optional)	1 tsp	2 tsp
Pepper	$^1/_4$ tsp	$^1/_2$ tsp
Salt to taste, depending on saltiness of smoked salmon.		

Choose large potatoes, preferably the same size.

Assemble all ingredients for the stuffing.

In the blender, combine smoked salmon, butter and cream until smooth.

Stuff potato skins with salmon mixture.

- Choose large potatoes, preferably the same size.
- Wash potatoes thoroughly and prick with a fork *(see page 39)*.
- Set potatoes on paper towels, as illustrated, and turn two or three times during cooking process.
- Place smoked salmon, butter, cream and chives in a blender and puree to smooth consistency.
- Season to taste with salt, pepper and lemon juice.
- When potatoes are done, let stand for a few minutes; slice lengthwise.
- Scoop out potato from skins and blend with smoked salmon mixture. Check seasoning.
- Fill potato skins with smoked salmon and potato mixture.
- Serve immediately; or set aside and reheat 2 minutes at HIGH just before seving.

This rich and savory entrée also makes a delicious main course served with a tossed green salad.

SALMON PIE

Servings	•4/5	• 6/7•
Setting	+ + +	+ + +
500 watts	min 24	min 30
600/650 watts	22	27
700 watts	18	23
Standing Time	8	12
Calories	440	
Fat Content	Average (30 g)	
Utensil: Bowl or ramekin	$1^1/2$ qt (1.5 l)	2 qt (2 l)
Ingredients		
Sliced salmon	15 oz (450 g)	24 oz (700 g)
Frozen spinach (defrosted)	10 oz (300 g)	15 oz (450 g)
Whipping cream	7 oz (200 g)	10 oz (300 g)
Grated cheddar	4 oz (120 g)	6 oz (180 g)
Lime juice	2 tbsp	3 tbsp
Grated nutmeg	$^1/4$ tsp	$^1/3$ tsp
Salt	$^1/2$ tsp	$^3/4$ tsp
Pepper	$^1/2$ tsp	$^3/4$ tsp
Puff pastry (thawed)	10 oz (300 g)	15 oz (450 g)

Remove the skin and bones from salmon slices.

Spread puff pastry evenly in bowl or ramekin, allowing ends of pastry to extend over the edge.

Prepare the mixture and spread evenly over pastry.

Bring flaps of pastry over mixture. Cut small hole in top of pastry and insert paper chimney to allow steam to escape.

- Remove the skin and bones from salmon slices.
- Roll out puff pastry into a square $^1/8''$ (3 mm) thick.
- Line inside of bowl or ramekin with clear plastic wrap *(see p. 22)*.
- Cover lining with pastry, allowing ends of pastry to extend over edge of container; the extra pastry will be used to cover the top of the pie.
- In a blender, coarsely chop the salmon and well-drained spinach with the cream and grated cheddar.
- Add lime juice, grated nutmeg, salt and pepper. Mix well to a smooth consistency.
- Spread salmon mixture evenly over the pastry and bring flaps of pastry over to cover mixture.
- Cut small hole in the pastry top and insert a paper tube to allow steam to escape during cooking.
- Place in the oven and cook as per indications on chart.

For lovely golden color, beat one egg with 2 tbsp soya sauce and brush over pastry.

Fish Tagiatelli

Servings	1	2
Setting	+ + +	+ + +
500 watts	min 2	min 3
600/650 watts	1¾	2½
700 watts	1½	2¼
Standing Time	2	2
Calories	330	
Fat Content	Low (11 g)	
Utensil: Rectangular au gratin dish	½ qt (0.5 l)	1 qt (1 l)
Ingredients		
Green tagiatelli, cooked	5 oz (150 g)	10 oz (300 g)
Fish filets	3 oz (100 g)	6 oz (200 g)
Asparagus tips, blanched	2 oz (60 g)	4 oz (120 g)
Small Green Onions with tops	1	2
Parsley	1 tbsp	2 tbsp
Lemon juice	1 tsp	2 tsp
Whipping cream	1 tbsp	2 tbsp
Olive oil	1 tsp	2 tsp
Pepper	⅛ tsp	¼ tsp
Salt	⅛ tsp	¼ tsp

Cook tagliatelli and blanch the asparagus tips.

Chop asparagus tips, parsley and onion. Cook fish filets with olive oil.

Mince fish and combine all ingredients with cream, salt and pepper.

- Cook tagliatelli as per chart on p. 198. Keep warm.
- Blanch asparagus as described on p. 36.
- Set fish filets in dish, sprinkle with oil and cook according to chart instructions.
- Chop asparagus tips, parsley and onion.
- When fish is cooked, mince it and sprinkle with lemon juice.
- Combine fish with chopped asparagus, parsley and onion.
- Pour cream over mixture; add salt and pepper and mix again.
- Serve on a bed of hot tagliatelli.

This deliciously aromatic entrée can also be served cold, as a salad. Simply add a sprinkling of oil and lemon juice prior to serving.

Crab Rolls

Servings	2	4
Setting	+ + +	+ + +
500 watts	min 4	min 6
600/650 watts	$3^1/2$	$5^1/4$
700 watts	3	$4^1/2$
Standing time	2	3
Calories	230	
Fat Content	Average (35 g)	
Utensil: Use paper towels.		
Ingredients		
Crab-flavored Fish Sticks or Crab Sticks	5	10
Thin slices of Bacon	5	10
Lettuce	1/2	1 small
Fresh mint leaves	10	20
Thin slices cucumber	10	20
Soya sauce	1/3 cup	2/3 cup
Vinegar	1 tbsp	2 tbsp
Water	1/3 tsp	2/3 tsp
Chopped garlic	1 tsp	2 tsp
Chopped chives	1 tbsp	2 tbsp
Pepper	1/4 tsp	1/2 tsp
Powdered ginger	1/4 tsp	1/2 tsp

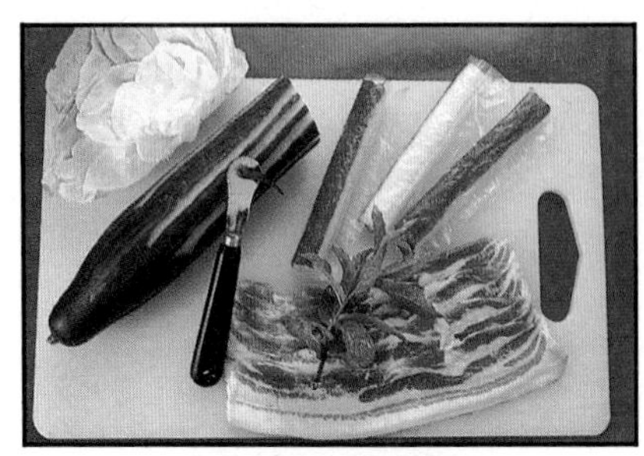

Prepare all ingredients: lettuce, crab fish sticks, bacon, mint and cucumber.

Wrap the crab fish sticks in thinly sliced bacon.

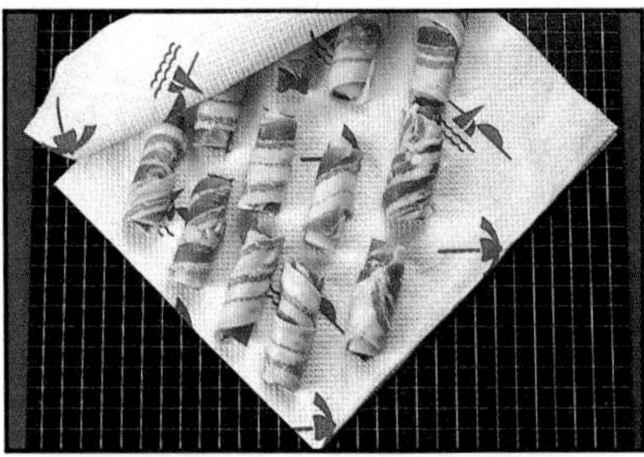

Cut the crab sticks in two and cook them between two sheets of paper towel.

- Wash, trim and separate lettuce leaves.
- Prepare cucumber, mint, garlic and chives.
- Wrap crab-flavored fish sticks or crab sticks in bacon slices. (The crab or fish sticks should be cut in two beforehand to make two small rolls with each.
- Place prepared crab rolls on paper towels in oven and cover with second sheet of paper towel. Cook according to directions on chart.
- Prepare sauce: Mix soya sauce, vinegar, water, garlic and chopped chives with pepper and powdered ginger.
- Let the fish rolls stand as per chart indications then serve as spring rolls, wrapped in lettuce leaves with a mint leaf and a slice of cucumber. Set out individual portions of sauce for each person.
- Vietnamese sauce lovers may replace half the soya sauce with nuoc-mâm.

This is an interesting way to serve the delicious fish sticks, usually of cod, flavored with crab. This dish can also be prepared with shelled crabmeat.

STUFFED PINEAPPLE

Servings	•2•	•4•
Setting	+ + +	+ + +
500 watts	min 5	min 8
600/650 watts	4 1/4	6 1/2
700 watts	3 3/4	6
Standing Time	3	4
Calories	275	
Fat Content	Low (16 g)	
Utensil: Use the pineapple shell.		
Ingredients		
Whole pineapple	1 small	1 medium
Crab meat	4 oz (120 g)	8 oz (240 g)
Slice(s) of ham	1	2
Sour cream	1/4 cup	1/2 cup
Chopped tarragon	1 tsp	2 tsp
Lemon juice	1 tbsp	2 tbsp
Paprika	1 tsp	2 tsp
Pepper	1/4 tsp	1/2 tsp
Salt	1/2 tsp	1 tsp

Empty pineapple into a dish to save the juice.

Chop the crab meat.

Cut pineapple and sliced ham into small cubes.

When the crab mixture is ready, fill the pineapple.

- Hollow out the pineapple, reserving the juice.
- Chop the crab meat.
- Cut pineapple and sliced ham into small cubes.
- Chop the tarragon.
- In a large bowl, mix pineapple, ham, crab meat and tarragon.
- Add sour cream, lemon juice, reserved pineapple juice, pepper, salt and half the paprika.
- Carefully blend the mixture.
- Cook and let stand as per chart directions.
- Use the pineapple as the serving dish.

This simple and deliciously appetizing stuffed pineapple is sure to entice you to try other variations.

Jumbo Shrimp Cocktail

Servings	1	2
Setting	++	++
500 watts	min 5	min 8
600/650 watts	4 1/4	6 1/2
700 watts	3 1/2	5 1/2
Standing Time	4	5 1/2
Calories	290	
Fat Content	Negligeable (3 g)	
Utensil: Round Dish	1/2 qt (0.5 l)	1 qt (1 l)
Ingredients		
Large shrimp	6 oz (170 g)	12 oz (340 g)
Tomato juice	1/4 cup	1/2 cup
Soya sauce	1 tbsp	2 tbsp
Vinegar	1 tbsp	2 tbsp
Powdered sugar	1 tbsp	2 tbsp
Chopped garlic	1 tsp	2 tsp
Tabasco sauce	2 drops	4 drops
Arrowroot	1 tsp	2 tsp
Salt	1/8 tsp	1/4 tsp

Lettuce leaves and lime slices to garnish.

Choose large shrimp of same size for more even cooking.

Shell and devein shrimp, leaving last ring and tail.

Prepare sauce and marinate shrimp for 1 hour.

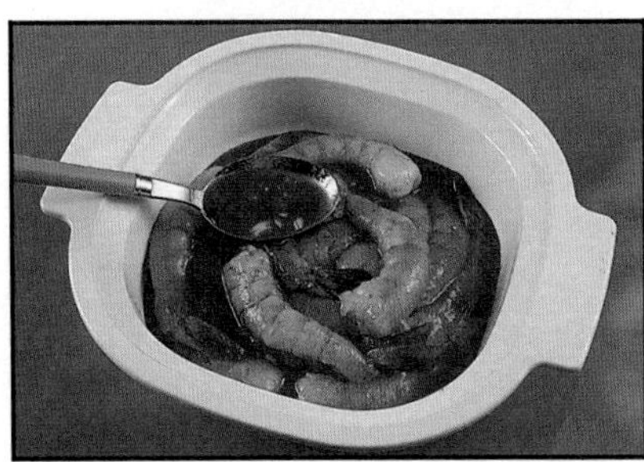

Make sure shrimp are well coated with sauce in cooking dish.

- Choose large shrimp, preferably the same size for even cooking.
- Shell and devein shrimp, leaving last ring and tail; the shrimp will be more attractive and easier to eat with fingers.
- To make sauce, mix tomato juice, soya sauce, vinegar, powdered sugar, chopped garlic, tabasco sauce, salt and arrowroot (mixed in a little water).
- Marinate shrimp for one hour in the refrigerator.
- Empty sauce into cooking dish and lay the shrimp in it; make sure shrimp are well covered in sauce.
- Cook and let stand as directed in chart.
- Refrigerate until ready to serve.
- Arrange shrimp in cocktail glass. Pour sauce in the center and decorate with lettuce leaf and lime wedge.

To add a more oriental flavor to this entrée, double the proportions of sugar, vinegar, soya sauce and tabasco.

Clams Escargot Style

Servings	1	2
Setting	+ + +	+ + +
500 watts	min $4^1/_4$	min $5^1/_2$
600/650 watts	$3^1/_2$	5
700 watts	3	4
Standing Time	1	2
Calories	390	
Fat Content	Moderately high (45 g)	
Utensil: Round Gratin Dish	6 in (15 cm)	9 in (22 cm)
Ingredients		
Clams, (size of a tablespoon)	9	18
Salted butter	2 oz (60 g)	4 oz (110 g)
Minced parsley	1 tsp	2 tsp
Minced chives	1 tsp	2 tsp
Minced tarragon	$^1/_2$ tsp	1 tsp
Minced shallot	1 tsp	2 tsp
Chopped garlic	$^1/_2$ tsp	1 tsp
Pepper	$^1/_4$ tsp	$^1/_2$ tsp
Lemon (optional)	$^1/_2$	1

Pry open clam shells with sharp knife.

Detach meat from the shell.

Prepare the escargot butter.

Serve piping hot with small escargot forks.

- Pry open clams with tip of sharp knife.
- Pull out upper valvule and detach clam meat from lower portion of shell.
- Arrange clams on cooking dish.
- In blender, combine salted butter, parsley, chives, tarragon, shallot and chopped garlic. Add pepper.
- Continue blending until smooth. This mixture is called "escargot butter".
- Put a dollop of this butter on each clam (see main photo).
- Set in oven to cook and let stand as per chart instructions. Serve piping hot; eat with escargot forks.
- Sprinkle with lemon juice to taste.

When made with the "butter" as described these clams are even tastier than regular escargots and cook perfectly in the microwave oven.

Bacon and Clam Salad

Servings	1	2
Setting	+ + +	+ + +
500 watts	min $5^1/2$	min $8^1/2$
600/650 watts	$4^3/4$	7
700 watts	4	6
Standing Time	3	4
Calories	375	
Fat Content	Average (38 g)	
Utensil: Paper Towels		
Ingredients		
Large clams	6	12
Bacon or smoked ham, sliced medium thick	6	12
Alfalfa sprouts or watercress	1 cup	2 cups
Olive oil	2 tbsp	4 tbsp
Wine vinegar	1/2 tbsp	1 tbsp
Pepper	1/8 tsp	1/4 tsp
Salt	1/8 tsp	1/4 tsp
Tomato and lemon rind to decorate		

Open the clam shells and remove meat from shells.

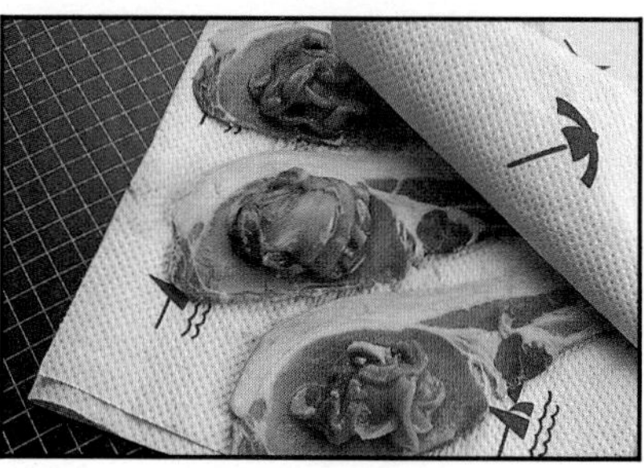

Arrange one clam on each bacon slice.

Prepare the dressing and pour over alfalfa sprout or watercress salad.

- Pry open clam shells with tip of sharp knife and pull out meat.
- Spread bacon (or ham) slices on paper towel and top each slice with clam. Cover each with paper towel.
- Cook and let stand according to chart instructions.
- Meanwhile, prepare dressing: beat together vinegar, salt, pepper and olive oil.
- When bacon and clam are cooked, set slices on a bed of alfalfa sprouts or watercress and pour on dressing.
- Decorate with lemon and tomato slices. You will enjoy the contrast between the crispy cool salad and the hot clam bacon combination.

Alfalfa sprouts, like watercress, make an unusually delicate salad. If you can't find either one, use any lettuce in season.

VELOUTÉ OF BABY CLAMS

Servings	•2/3	• 4/5•
Setting	+ + then + + +	+ + then + + +
500 watts	min 10 + 5	min 16 + 8
600/650 watts	8 + 4 1/2	14 + 7
700 watts	7 + 4	12 + 6
Standing Time	4	6
Calories	250	
Fat Content	Low (14 g)	
Utensil: 2 bowls	1 1/2 qt (1.5 l)	3 qt (3 l)
Ingredients		
Canned baby clams (or mussels)	1 small	1 large
Egg yolks	2	4
Milk	1 cup	2 cups
Dry white wine	1/2 cup	1 cup
Water	1/2 cup	1 cup
Lemon juice	1 tbsp	2 tbsp
Whipping cream	2 tbsp	4 tbsp
Minced chives	1 tbsp	2 tbsp
Salt	1/4 tsp	1/2 tsp
Pepper	1/4 tsp	1/2 tsp

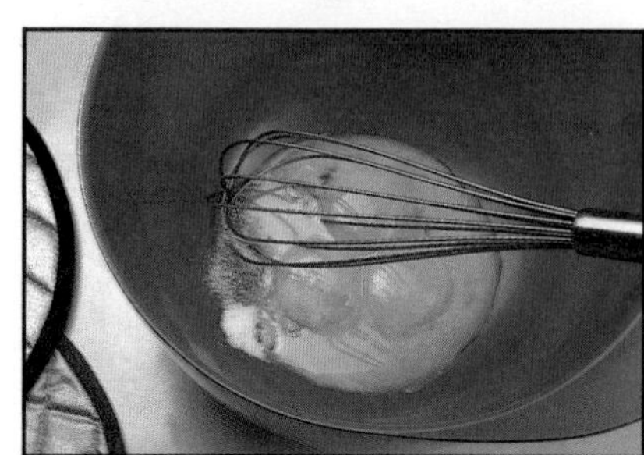

Beat egg yolks in bowl with salt and pepper.

Add milk, white wine, water and clam juice and beat rapidly.

After the first cooking period, put mixture through sieve and pour into a second bowl.

Pour in cream, lemon juice and clams.

- Beat egg yolks, salt and pepper in a bowl.
- Pour milk, white wine and water into the egg mixture. Add the clam juice and beat rapidly.
- Cook in the oven at MEDIUM level for the first cooking time indicated on the chart.
- Beat the mixture again and pour through a sieve. Transfer to a second cooking bowl.
- Add cream, lemon juice and clams to the mixture. Adjust seasoning.
- Beat again to mix thoroughly. Return to oven for second cooking phase at HIGH.
- Let stand for period indicated on chart then serve, sprinkled with chopped chives.

Of course, this creamy soup will taste even better if prepared with fresh clams!

PEASANT SOUP

Servings	4	8
Setting	+ + +	+ + +
500 watts	min 35	min 50
600/650 watts	32	45
700 watts	30	42
Standing time	6	8
Calories	400	
Fat Content	Average (33 g)	
Utensil: Deep, round dish	$2^{1}/_{2}$ qt (2.5 l)	5 qt (5 l)
Ingredients		
Carrots	1/3 lb (150 g)	2/3 lb (300 g)
Zucchini	1/3 lb (150 g)	2/3 lb (300 g)
Celery	1/3 lb (150 g)	2/3 lb (300 g)
Turnip	1/3 lb (150 g)	2/3 lb (300 g)
Thickly sliced ham	4 oz (120 g)	8 oz (240 g)
Gruyère cheese	4 oz (120 g)	8 oz (240 g)
Minced shallot	2 tbsp	4 tbsp
Minced garlic	1 tsp	2 tsp
Chopped parsley	1 tbsp	2 tbsp
Butter	2 oz (60 g)	4 oz (120 g)
Whipping cream	1 tbsp	2 tbsp
Chicken stock	4 cups	8 cups
Pepper	1/2 tsp	1 tsp
Salt	1/2 tsp	1 tsp

Cut vegetables, ham and gruyère cheese into small cubes.

Sauté shallots, garlic and minced parsley in butter.

Add cubed vegetables, ham and gruyère.

Pour in chicken stock, add seasoning and stir.

- Wash and trim all vegetables.
- Cut carrots, zucchini, celery, turnip, ham and gruyère into small cubes.
- Mince shallot, garlic and parsley.
- Put butter, minced shallot, garlic and parsley into cooking dish.
- Cook on HIGH for 3 minutes.
- Add cubed vegetables, ham and gruyère to cooking dish and continue cooking for 5 minutes, stirring often.
- Pour heated chicken stock over vegetables, (cold stock would interrupt the cooking process) and add 15 minutes to actual cooking time.
- Add salt and pepper to taste and stir.
- Cover dish and cook for the rest of the time directed on chart, stirring often.
- Add cream and check seasoning at the end of cooking time. Serve immediately after indicated standing time.

This delicious old-fashioned soup tastes as if it simmered all night over an open fire, but takes only minutes.

Caution: It is a good idea to cook soups in a bowl twice the size necessary to hold the ingredients, especially if the recipe calls for milk.

Cream of corn

Servings	2	4
Setting	+ + + then + +	+ + + then + +
500 watts	min 7 + 20	min 7 + 30
600/650 watts	7 + 18	7 + 27
700 watts	7 + 16	7 + 24
Standing Time	4	6
Calories	410	
Fat Content	Quite Low (21 g)	
Utensil: Bowl	1 1/2 qt (1.5 l)	3 qt (3 l)
Ingredients		
Corn niblets	2 cups	4 cups
Large red peppers	2	4
Whipping cream	1/2 cup	1 cup
Chicken stock	2 cups	4 cups
Lemon	1/2	1
Chopped chives (optional)	1 tbsp	2 tbsp
Pepper	1/4 tsp	1/2 tsp
Salt	1/4 tsp	1/2 tsp

Cut peppers in two and cook in microwave for 7 minutes; they will peel easily.

Crush the corn niblets in the blender and add preheated chicken stock.

Pour the stock through a sieve. Purée the peeled peppers until creamy.

- Cut the peppers in half and cook in the microwave at HIGH for 7 minutes on paper towels.
- Meanwhile, crush the corn niblets in the blender.
- Add chicken stock (heated) to the crushed niblets. Blend well and run through the sieve (*see p. 29*) to strain out niblet skins.
- Pour in half the cream. Add salt and pepper to taste.
- When the peppers are done, put the corn stock in the microwave and cook according to chart directions on MEDIUM.
- Peel and remove seeds from peppers (This is simple once they have been cooked.)
- Put peeled peppers with lemon juice in blender and purée until creamy. Add cayenne pepper or two drops of tabasco sauce to taste.
- When the stock is ready, pour it once more through the sieve. Add the other half of the cream and mixed chives. Stir.
- Mix well with pureed pepper mixture and serve.

This classic recipe from the U.S. South has been deliciously adapted for microwave cooking.

Homemade Onion Soup

Servings	• 1	• 2 •
Setting	+ + +	+ + +
500 watts	min 6 + 18	min 8 + 22
600/650 watts	6 + 16	8 + 20
700 watts	6 + 14	8 + 18
Standing time	None	None**
Calories	380*	
Fat Content	Low (18 g)	
Utensil: Round Gratin Dish	6 in (15 cm)	8 in (20 cm)
Ingredients		
Thinly sliced onion	1 cup	2 cups
Minced garlic	1 tsp	2 tsp
Beef stock or bouillon	1 cup	2 cups
Dry white wine	1/4 cup	1/2 cup
Minced parsley	1 tbsp	2 tbsp
Grated gruyère	1/4 cup	1/2 cup
French bread, sliced	2	4
Pepper	1/2 tsp	1 tsp
Salt	1/4 tsp	1/2 tsp

* Halving the quantity of gruyère cheese and eliminating the bread makes this recipe suitable for a calorie-reduced diet (less than 100 calories per serving and no fat). Although not so rich or substantial as the original, it is still delicious.

** We have eliminated the standing time because the cheese topping tends to become hard and rubbery when it becomes cold.

Peel onion and garlic; heat the beef bouillon.

Thinly slice onion; mince garlic and parsley. Put all ingredients in gratin dish.

Add preheated bouillon and white wine to cooked onion.

Add chopped parsley, bread slices and grated gruyère 5 minutes before end of cooking process.

- Peel the onions and garlic.
- Thinly slice the onions; mince the garlic and parsley.
- Put onions, garlic and spoonful of stock in gratin dish. Cook on HIGH for first cooking period on chart.
- Add the preheated beef stock.
- Add white wine, salt and half the pepper.
- Stir and cook for the second cooking period directed on chart. Five minutes before end of cooking, add bread, parsley, and remaining pepper.
- Sprinkle with cheese and finish cooking.
- Served as a first course, or to end off a festive night, a good bowl of onion soup acts as an aid to digestion.

Many recipes suggest making onion soup in a large deep bowl. We much prefer individual gratin bowls.

Raclette San Daniele

Servings	1	2
Setting	+ + +	+ + +
500 watts	min $4^1/_2$	min 6
600/650 watts	4	6
700 watts	$3^1/_2$	5
Standing time	None	None*
Calories	480	
Fat Content	Reasonably High (42 g)	
Utensil: Paper Towel		
Ingredients		
Thin slices of Raclette cheese	2	4
Thin slices of smoked ham	2	4
Medium-thick slices toasted bread	2	4
Sweet and sour pickles	2	4
Paprika	$^1/_2$ tsp	1 tsp
Freshly ground pepper	A dash per slice	

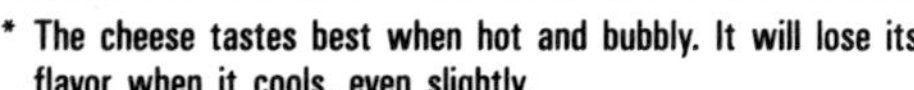

* The cheese tastes best when hot and bubbly. It will lose its flavor when it cools, even slightly.

Toast bread. Ask the butcher to cut thin slices of ham.

Slice raclette cheese into $^1/_8$ in (3 mm) slices. Cut off rind.

Arrange ham, and cheese on bread; decorate with pickles.

- Toast bread in toaster or microwave oven (*see p. 37*).
- Slice raclette cheese into $^1/_8$ in (3 mm) slices. Pare off the rind.
- Arrange one slice ham and one slice raclette cheese on each slice of toast.
- Top with chopped sweet and sour pickle.
- Sprinkle with paprika. Add a dash of freshly ground pepper. Do not add salt. Cheese and ham contain enough.
- Cook in microwave oven on paper towel according to chart indications. Serve immediately.
- Serve two slices per person as an entrée; increase portions and serve with tossed green salad for a main course.

This raclette is adapted from a recipe originating in Northern Italy; it is usually prepared with the famous San Daniele ham.

HAM CROISSANTS

Servings	1	2
Setting	+ + +	+ + +
500 watts	min 3 1/2	min 6
600/650 watts	3	5
700 watts	2 1/2	4
Standing time	2	3
Calories	580	
Fat Content	Quite High (41 g)	
Utensil: Paper Towels		
Ingredients		
Croissants	1	2
Cooked ham	2 oz (60 g)	4 oz (120 g)
Whipping cream	1 tsp	2 tsp
Mayonnaise	1 tbsp	2 tbsp
Ketchup	1 tsp	2 tsp
Grated cheese	1 tbsp	2 tbsp
Hot mustard	1 tsp	2 tsp
Chopped parsley	1 tsp	2 tsp
Paprika	1/4 tsp	1/2 tsp
Pepper	1/8 tsp	1/4 tsp
Salt	1/8 tsp	1/4 tsp

Put diced ham along with all other ingredients into blender.

Purée mixture until reasonably smooth.

Split croissants in two lengthwise and garnish with the purée.

- Coarsely dice the ham
- Put diced ham, cream, mayonnaise, ketchup, grated cheese, hot mustard, chopped parsley, paprika, salt and pepper into blender and process until mixture is reasonably smooth.
- Split croissants in two lengthwise and spread pureed mixture on them.
- Cook in microwave oven on paper towels according to chart instructions.
- Let stand and serve with a lettuce salad.

This simple yet delectable recipe is a unique approach to a fast-and-easy meal.

HAWAIIAN GRATIN

Servings	• 1	• 2 •
Setting	+ + +	+ + +
500 watts	min 3	min 5
600/650 watts	3	5
700 watts	2 1/2	4
Standing time	2	3
Calories	430	
Fat Content	Moderate (33 g)	
Utensil: Round Gratin Dish	6 in (15 cm)	8 in (20 cm)
Ingredients		
Pineapple slices	1	2
Cooked Ham	2 oz (60 g)	4 oz (120 g)
Red pepper	1/4	1/2
Green pepper	1/4	1/2
Pistachio nuts, shelled	1 tsp	2 tsp
Grated parmesan	1 tbsp	2 tbsp
Whipping cream	1 tbsp	2 tbsp
Arrowroot or cornstarch	1 tsp	2 tsp
Pepper	1/4 tsp	1/2 tsp
Salt	1/8 tsp	1/4 tsp

The ingredients for this simple recipe should be good quality and perfectly fresh, especially the pineapple.

Peel the pineapple and slice it. Cut peppers into small cubes and ham into thin slivers.

Mix all ingredients in a bowl.

Arrange pineapple slices in a gratin dish and garnish with ham mixture.

- Peel and slice pineapple reserve the juice.
- Mix the cornstarch or arrowroot with pineapple juice.
- Cut peppers into small cubes and ham into thin slivers.
- Combine cubed peppers, slivered ham, pistachios, grated parmesan, cream, pepper and salt in a bowl.
- Add cornstarch (or arrowroot) mixture. Stir well to mix.
- Arrange pineapple slices in gratin dish.
- Spread ham mixture over pineapple.
- Cover with wax paper and cook in microwave as per chart instructions.
- Serve very hot, immediately after standing time is complete.

Pineapple, a delectable and nutritious fruit, adds a hawaiian aroma to this gratin dish. Hawaii, by the way, was once called the "Sandwich Islands"!

Stuffed Peppers

Servings	• 1 •	2 •
Setting	+ + +	+ + +
	min	min
500 watts	11	20
600/650 watts	10	18
700 watts	9	16
Standing time	5	7

Calories	200	
Fat Content	Low (16 g)	
Utensil: Dish or Serving Plate		
Ingredients		
Medium size green pepper(s)	1	2
Medium size red or yellow pepper(s)	1	2
Sausage meat	1 oz (30 g)	2 oz (60 g)
Bread, trimmed of crust, dipped in milk	1/4 cup	1/2 cup
Whipping cream	1 tsp	2 tsp
Chopped parsley	1/2 tbsp	1 tbsp
Chopped basil	1 tsp	2 tsp
Chopped garlic	1/2 tsp	1 tsp
Lemon juice	1 tsp	2 tsp
Pepper	1/4 tsp	1/2 tsp
Salt	1/8 tsp	1/4 tsp
Olive oil	A dash per pepper	

Select very fresh, well-shaped peppers of identical size.

Coarsely chop red and yellow peppers. Soak bread in milk.

Stuff green peppers with mixture.

- Select green peppers of identical size, as regularly-shaped as possible. (The shape of the red or yellow peppers is not important — they are used for the stuffing only.)
- Coarsely chop red and yellow peppers. Remove seeds, white membranes and the stem. Soak the bread in a little milk to soften.
- In a blender, prepare stuffing with red and yellow pepper cubes, sausage meat, bread, cream, parsley, basil, garlic, lemon juice, salt and pepper. Stuffing should be smooth-textured.
- Cut the tops off the green peppers, clean out the seeds and stuff with mixture. Replace the tops of peppers.
- Arrange stuffed peppers in plate or serving dish. Dribble a little olive oil on each pepper and cook in microwave as per chart instructions.

Make sure that peppers stand upright in the dish. If necessary, set them in a bed of coarse salt.

Stuffed Crêpes À la Bretonne

Servings	• 1	• 2 •
Setting	+ + +	+ + +
500 watts	min 3	min 5
600/650 watts	$2^1/2$	4
700 watts	$2^1/4$	$3^1/2$
Standing Time	2	3
Calories	305	
Fat Content	Low (16 g)	
Utensil: Bowl	1 qt (1 l)	$1^1/2$ qt (1.5 l)
Ingredients		
Unsweetened crêpe(s)	1	2
Small peeled shrimp	$^1/4$ cup	$^1/2$ cup
Small cultivated mushrooms	$^1/4$ cup	$^1/2$ cup
Grated cheese	2 tbsp	4 tbsp
Cooked rice	2 tbsp	4 tbsp
Cocktail sauce	2 tbsp	4 tbsp
Paprika	$^1/4$ tsp	$^1/2$ tsp
Chopped chives	1 tsp	2 tsp
Pepper	$^1/4$ tsp	$^1/2$ tsp
Salt	$^1/8$ tsp	$^1/4$ tsp
Lemon	$^1/4$	$^1/2$

Prepare crêpes in a frying pan. Microwave ovens are not suited to cooking crêpes.

Gently stir all stuffing ingredients in a microwave-safe bowl.

Spread stuffing mixture on the crêpes and roll them up.

- Buy ready-made crêpes or prepare them in a frying pan. They are one of the few things that cannot be properly made in a microwave.
- Wash the mushrooms, slice very thinly, and sprinkle with lemon juice to avoid darkening.
- Drain the shrimp. Mince chives.
- Gently combine shrimp, mushrooms, grated cheese, cooked rice, cocktail sauce, paprika, minced chives, salt and pepper in a large bowl.
- Cook in microwave as indicated on the chart.
- Lay the crêpes on a work surface, top with the cooked filling and gently roll them up.
- If necessary, reheat on HIGH, 1 minute per crêpe.

Shrimp, cheese and mushrooms are a delicious combination, especially in this savory dish from Brittany.

Gourmet mushrooms

Servings	1	2
Setting	+ + +	+ + +
500 watts	min 4	min 7
600/650 watts	$3^1/_2$	$6^1/_2$
700 watts	3	6
Standing Time	2	3
Calories	200	
Fat Content	Low (13 g)	

Utensil: Deep casserole cover or gratin dish

Ingredients		
Large mushrooms	2	4
Egg(s)	1	2
Grated cheese	1 tbsp	2 tbsp
Tomato(es), medium size	1	2
Chopped shallot	1 tbsp	2 tbsp
Chopped garlic	1 tbsp	2 tbsp
Chopped herbs, (parsley, tarragon, chives, etc.)	1 tbsp	2 tsp
Pepper	$^1/_4$ tsp	$^1/_2$ tsp
Salt	$^1/_4$ tsp	$^1/_2$ tsp
Soya Sauce	Enough to baste mushrooms	

Choose well-shaped mushrooms with large caps.

Gently remove stems; clean and wash them.

Baste mushroom caps with soya sauce. Chop stems.

Arrange mushroom caps in a circle in gratin dish and stuff them.

- Choose well-shaped mushrooms with large rounded caps.
- Gently pull off stems.
- Wash caps and scrub stems to elminiate all dirt and sand particles.
- Baste mushroom caps with soya sauce. This will prevent them from oxydizing and will help them to take on a lovely golden coloring during cooking.
- Chop mushroom stems, shallots, garlic and herbs. Crush tomato pulp.
- Prepare stuffing: Blend eggs, grated cheese, tomato pulp, shallots, garlic, herbs, chopped mushroom stems, salt and pepper.
- Arrange mushroom caps in a circle in gratin dish and fill with stuffing.
- Cook in microwave according to chart directions.
- Half-way through cooking, pour out excess mushroom juice and return to oven.

A light and sophisticated entrée that is as quick to prepare as mushrooms grow!

HAM SOUFFLE

Servings	• 1	• 2*•
Setting	+ and ++	+ and ++
500 watts	min 20	min 30
600/650 watts	18	26
700 watts	17	24
Standing Time**	None	None
Calories	520	
Fat Content	Quite High (41 g)	
Utensil: Ramekin*	Single	Double
Ingredients		
Cooked ham	3 oz (80 g)	6 oz (160 g)
Whipping cream	1 tbsp	2 tbsp
Eggs	2	4
Flour	2 tbsp	4 tbsp
Milk	2 tbsp	4 tbsp
Chopped tarragon	1 tsp	2 tsp
Chopped shallot	1 tsp	2 tsp
Grated cheese	1 tbsp	2 tbsp
Pepper	1/4 tsp	1/2 tsp
Salt	1/8 tsp	1/4 tsp

* Soufflés turn out better when cooked in single-serving or double-serving ramekins. For 3 or more servings, prepare multiples of a single or double serving to cook at the same time. But dont try to cook more than 6 servings at once.

** Soufflés fall almost immediately so no standing time is required.

Finely chop ham. Separate eggs. Blend flour into milk.

Stir all ingredients together very gently.

Add grated cheese. Whip egg whites into peaks.

Fold egg whites into other ingredients very gently.

- Chop the ham finely.
- Separate the eggs.
- Incorporate flour into milk.
- Blend ham, cream, egg yolks, flour mixture, tarragon, shallots, salt and pepper; stir gently.
- Add grated cheese. Stir gently.
- Add a pinch of salt to egg whites and whip to form stiff peaks.
- Gently fold egg whites into ham mixture, being careful not to alter the texture of the egg whites.
- Pour into ramekin dish(es).
- Cook in microwave according to chart instructions, starting at LOW then resetting at MEDIUM, midway through cooking.
- Serve immediately.

Some recipes call for more flour which results in a higher but heavier soufflé.

EGGS À LA POULETTE

Servings	1	2
Setting	+ +	+ +
500 watts	min 3	min $4^{1}/_{2}$
600/650 watts	$2^{3}/_{4}$	4
700 watts	$2^{1}/_{2}$	$3^{1}/_{2}$
Standing Time	$1^{1}/_{2}$	2
Calories	370	
Fat Content	Average (32 g)	
Utensil: individual ramekin	1	2
Ingredients		
Eggs	2	4
Butter	$^{1}/_{2}$ tsp	1 tsp
Whipping cream	$^{1}/_{4}$ cup	$^{1}/_{2}$ cup
Curry	$^{1}/_{2}$ tsp	1 tsp
Pepper	$^{1}/_{4}$ tsp	$^{1}/_{2}$ tsp
Salt	$^{1}/_{4}$ tsp	$^{1}/_{2}$ tsp

Use only very fresh eggs.

Butter bottom and sides of ramekins.

Break two eggs into each ramekin.

Add curried cream.

- Use only fresh eggs for this recipe.
- Butter bottom and sides of ramekins.
- Mix cream with curry, salt and pepper.
- Break two eggs into each ramekin and pierce the yolks *(see p. 39)*.
- Pour curried cream over eggs and cover.
- Cook in microwave as per chart instructions. Be sure to foldow cooking times to the letter!*.
- After standing time, serve in the ramekins. This dish is best eaten with a spoon.

* *If the eggs seem a little underdone, leave then in the oven for a few more seconds. However, if they seem just right, forget the standing time which is, as we explained in the introduction, an extra cooking period.*

An extremely simple and economical dish with great taste.

SCRAMBLED EGGS WITH ASPARAGUS TIPS

Servings	• 1 •	2 •
Setting	+ + +	+ + +
	min	min
500 watts	2	3 3/4
600/650 watts	1 3/4	3 1/4
700 watts	1 1/2	3
Standing Time	2	2 1/2
Calories	310	
Fat Content	Reasonably Low (25 g)	
Utensil: Bowl	1/2 qt (0.5 l)	1 qt (1 l)
Ingredients		
Eggs	2	4
Melted butter	1 tsp	2 tsp
Asparagus tips, cooked	5	10
Whipping cream	1 tbsp	2 tbsp
Milk	2 tbsp	4 tbsp
Pepper	1/4 tsp	1/2 tsp
Salt	1/4 tsp	1/2 tsp

Cook the asparagus as indicated in the recipe on p. 86.

Crack eggs into a bowl, and beat.

Add cream, milk, salt and pepper. Stir, then add cooked sliced asparagus tips.

- Cook asparagus according to instructions on p. 86.
- White, purple, green or even wild asparagus (in season) can be used in this recipe. You can also use canned asparagus.
- Crack eggs into a bowl and beat them. For creamier eggs, pass them through a sieve *(see p. 29)*.
- Add cream, milk, salt and pepper and stir.
- Add cooked asparagus tips, cut in two.
- Melt butter in a bowl in the microwave for 1 minute on HIGH. Pour the asparagus mixture into the melted butter.
- Cook in the microwave as per chart instructions, covered with a sheet of wax paper.
- Stir half-way through the cooking process.
- Let stand for complete standing time before serving.

Since individual tastes differ, those who like their eggs runnier might want to reduce cooking and standing times.

Asparagus Mousseline

Servings		• 2 •	• 4 •
Setting:	Asparagus	+ + +	+ + +
	Sauce	+ +	+ +
500 watts:	Asparagus	12	18
	Sauce	3 1/2	5
600/650 watts:	Asparagus	11	17
	Sauce	3	4 1/2
700 watts:	Asparagus	10	16
	Sauce	2 3/4	4
Standing Time:	Asparagus	4	6
	Sauce	None	None

Calories	320	
Fat Content	Quite low (27 g)	
Utensil: Rectangular dish, and bowl or ramekin	1 1/2 qt* 1/2 qt*	2 1/2 qt* 1 qt*
Ingredients		
Asparagus	1 lb (450 g)	2 lbs (900 g)
Hot water	1/4 cup	1/4 cup
Salt	1/2 tsp	1 tsp
Butter	1 tbsp	2 tbsp
Whipping cream	1/2 cup	1 cup
Egg yolk(s)	1	2
Lemon juice	1 tsp	2 tsp
Hot French mustard	1 tbsp	2 tbsp
Pepper	1/4 tsp	1/2 tsp
Salt	1/4 tsp	1/2 tsp

* 1/2 qt = (0.5 l)
1 qt = (1 l)
1 1/2 qt = (1.5 l)
2 1/2 qt = (2.5 l)

Clean and pare asparagus.

Set asparagus in dish with hot water and salt.

For the mousseline sauce, add egg yolks, lemon juice and half the cream to melted butter.

Half way through cooking process, add mustard and the rest of the cream. Stir.

- Clean and pare asparagus.
- Set asparagus in dish with hot water and salt.
- Cover and cook in microwave as per chart instructions.
- While asparagus is standing, prepare mousseline sauce. Begin by melting butter for 1 minute in microwave set on HIGH.
- Add lightly beaten egg yolks, lemon juice, pepper, salt and half the cream. Cover.
- Cook in microwave according to chart instructions.
- Half-way through cooking process, add mustard and the rest of the cream. Stir. Complete cooking uncovered.
- Drain the asparagus and cover with mousseline sauce.

If mousseline sauce should curdle or separate, rescue it by following directions on p. 29.

Greek Appetizers

Servings	•2/3	• 4/5•
Setting	+ + +	+ + +
500 watts	min 8	min 12
600/650 watts	7 1/2	11
700 watts	7	10
Standing Time	10 + 2 hours refrigerated	10
Calories	310	
Fat Content	Low (15 g)	
Utensil: Deep, Round Dish	2 qt (2 l)	3 qt (3 l)
Ingredients		
Canned small mushrooms	1/2 cup	1 cup
Black olives	1/4 cup	1/2 cup
Canned small onions	1/2 cup	1 cup
Canned cauliflower	1/2 cup	1 cup
Tomato juice	1/4 cup	1/2 cup
Vinegar	2 tbsp	4 tbsp
Lemon juice	1 tbsp	2 tbsp
Powdered sugar	2 tbsp	4 tbsp
Chopped parsley	1 tbsp	2 tbsp
Coriander seeds	1 tsp	2 tsp
Cornstarch or arrowroot	2 tsp	4 tsp
Tabasco sauce	4 drops	8 drops
Olive oil	1 tbsp	2 tbsp
Salt	1/4 tsp	1/2 tsp
Dry white wine	2 tbsp	4 tbsp

For the sauce, mix tomato juice, vinegar, lemon juice, sugar, parsley, coriander seed, Tabasco and salt.

Drain the mushrooms, onions and cauliflower. Pit the olives.

Toss the vegetables and olives and cover with sauce. Incorporate cornstarch or arrowroot into wine.

- Prepare sauce by mixing tomato juice, vinegar, lemon juice, powdered sugar, chopped parsley, coriander seeds, tabasco sauce and salt.
- Drain mushrooms, onion, and cauliflower.
- Pit olives or buy unpitted olives.
- Toss vegetables and olives in the cooking dish.
- Pour sauce over mixture.
- Sprinkle with olive oil.
- Dilute cornstarch or arrowroot in white wine and pour over mixture. Stir.
- Cover dish and cook in microwave according to chart instructions.
- Stir often during cooking process.
- Let stand and chill before serving.

This recipe, adapted from Greek cuisine, is even more authentic with the addition of a few drops of the Greek aniseed liqueur called Ouzo into the sauce.

Fish, Shellfish and Crustaceans

Cooking Chart

FOOD	WEIGHT	COOKING TIME (MIN) 500W	600/650W	700W	SETTING
FISH					
Filets, thin, (¼ in or 7 mm)	1 lb (450 g)	5 min	4½ min	4 min	+ + +
Filets, medium, (½ in or 14 mm)	1 lb (450 g)	6½ min	5¾ min	5 min	+ + +
Filets, thick, (1 in or 28 mm)	1 lb (450 g)	9 min	8 min	7 min	+ + +
Steaks, medium, thick (½ in or 14 mm)	1 lb (450 g)	7½ min	6½ min	6 min	+ + +
Steaks, thick, (1 in or 28 mm)	1 lb (450 g)	10 min	9 min	8 min	+ + +
Whole fish	2 lb (900 g)	15 min	13½ min	12 min	+ + +
SHELLFISH					
Clams	6 large	5 min	4½ min	4 min	+ + +
Scallops or Coquilles St. Jacques	1 lb (450 g)	5 min	4½ min	4 min	+ + +
	or	9 min	8 min	7 min	+ +
SEAFOOD					
Crab (legs)	1 lb (450 g)	6 min	5½ min	5 min	+ + +
Lobster tails or Scampi	1 lb (450 g)	6 min	5½ min	5 min	+ + +
Lobster, whole	2 lb (900 g)	10 min	9 min	8 min	+ + +
Shrimp, peeled	1 lb (450 g)	6 min	5½ min	5 min	+ +
Shrimp, unpeeled	1 lb (450 g)	7 min	6½ min	6 min	+ + +

For fragile filets return to oven one third of the way through cooking and let stand 5 minutes before serving.

"Filets" are pieces of fish cut with the grain of the meat i.e. cut parallel to the spine.

"Steaks" are slices of fish cut against the meat's grain i.e. perpendicular to the spine.

If you compare to beef, filets ressemble to scallops and steaks look like tournedos.

Preparing Fish

More and more often, cooks buy their fish already cleaned and prepared for cooking. However, if you happen to find yourself with a fresh whole fish on your hands, it would be a shame if you didn't know how to prepare it yourself.

You will add to your reputation as a chef if you know how to gut a fish, and properly remove the scales and fins.

Take, for example, these two fresh walleye or perch, weighing about 1 lb (450 g) each.

First, you have to remove the scales, using either a special scaler or an ordinary sharp knife.

The scales always have to be removed from the tail towards the head. Run your fingers lightly over the skin to make sure all the scales are removed.

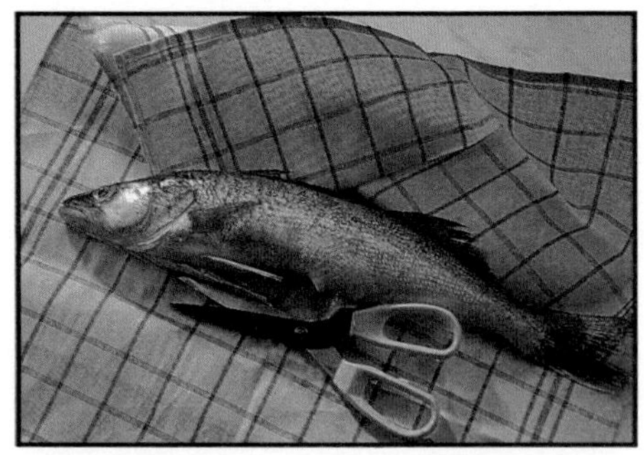

The next step is to gut the fish. With scissors, cut along the belly of the fish starting at the opening just under the tail and finishing under the gills. Use kitchen gloves to pull out the innards. Rinse the inside of the fish several times under cold running water.

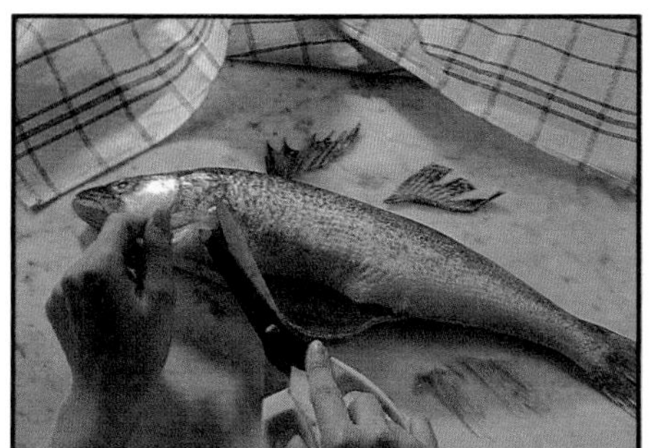

Dry the fish. Rinse your scissors, and then cut off the fins and any spines.

The fish is now ready to be cooked whole. Prepare the second fish the same way.

Can You Scale Fish in the Sink?
You should not scale fish in the sink unless it is equipped with a garbage disposal. Fish scales tend to clog up the drains otherwise. It is far better to work on a flat surface that can be cleaned easily.

How Do You Make Filets?
Fileting fish is not particularly complicated, but you have to work with a very long, sharp, and flexible knife.

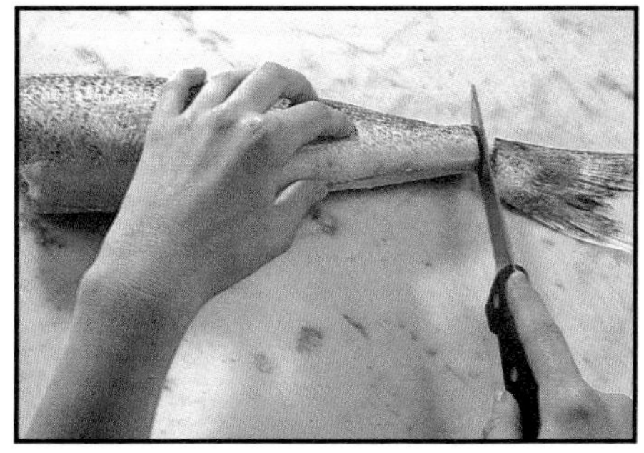

After having prepared the whole fish as just shown, cut off the head and the tail.

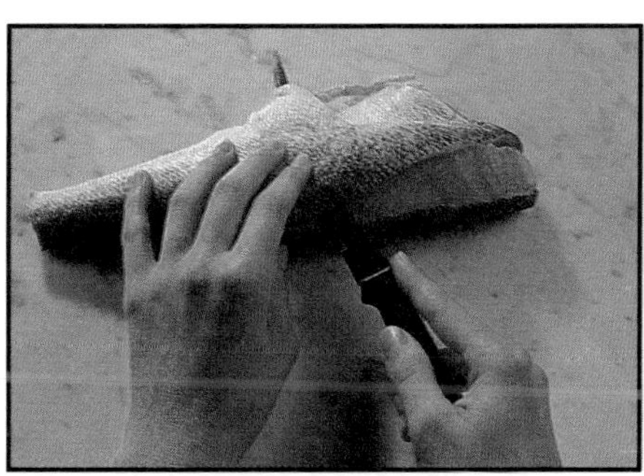

Slide the knife along the backbone from the head towards the tail. With your other hand, apply light pressure to the top side of the fish. You should be able to feel the backbone through the flesh so that you can cut smoothly along its length.

Turn the fish over and remove the other filet the same way.

Is Fish Skin Edible?
Yes, for certain fish such as trout, salmon and even sole. It's a question of personal taste. In any case, the skin is always far tastier when it's brown and crispy, which is hard to do in the microwave oven. As a general rule, therefore, it is better to remove the skin when preparing filets of fish.

Place the filet skin-side-down on the work surface. Using uniform pressure, slide the knife under the skin from the tail towards the head, keeping the blade almost parallel to the skin. With the fingers of your other hand, apply pressure on the flesh just in front of the blade; this will help you guide the knife more accurately. If you find that too much flesh is left on the skin, angle the knife blade down a little. If you find that the skin is tearing, angle the blade up a bit. It is a question of touch, which will improve with practice.

How Long Does It Take to Prepare a Fish?
At first it will take you about 15 minutes, but after a little experience, you will be able to do it in less than 5.

Fish filets with leeks

Servings	•1	•2•
Setting	+ + +	+ + +
500 watts	min 10	min 13
600/650 watts	9	12
700 watts	8 1/2	11
Standing Time	5	5
Calories	320	
Fat Content	Low (11 g)	
Utensil: Deep Dish with steamer and oval cooking dish	1/2 qt* 6 in*	1 qt* 8 in*
Ingredients		
Fish filets, medium thick	8 oz (225 g)	1 lb (450 g)
Small leeks	2	4
Chopped shallots	1 tbsp	2 tbsp
Crushed garlic	1 tsp	2 tsp
Butter	1 tsp	2 tsp
Lemon juice	1 tsp	2 tsp
Dry white wine	1 tbsp	2 tbsp
Paprika	1/2 tsp	1 tsp
Pepper	1/4 tsp	1/2 tsp
Salt	1/4 tsp	1/2 tsp
Oil	A few drops to sear the filets	

* 1/2 qt = (0.5 l)
1 qt = (1 l)
6 in = (15 cm)
8 in = (20 cm)

Purchase fish already fileted, or prepare as indicated on pp 92 and 93.

Wash leeks. Slice white and pale green portions into thin rounds.

Arrange leeks, shallots, garlic, butter, lemon juice, white wine salt and pepper in the cooking dish.

Cook the leeks on the top shelf and the fish filets in the bottom section of the microwave.

- Purchase fish already fileted, or prepare as indicated on pp. 92 and 93.
- The best fish for this recipe are pike, perch, plaice, sole and mackerel.
- Wash leeks. Cut white and pale green sections into thin round strips. Reserve dark green portion for other uses (such as soup base).
- Chop shallots and crush garlic.
- Place sliced leeks along with shallots, garlic, butter, lemon juice, white wine, salt and pepper in oval cooking dish.
- Grease fish filets with oil and set on steamer over the round dish; pour 1/4 cup of water in the bottom.
- Cook leeks on the upper shelf of the microwave and fish on the bottom section as per chart instructions.
- Take filets out of the microwave 5 minutes before end of cooking time and let stand while the leeks finish cooking.
- Serve filets sprinkled with paprika on a bed of leeks.

Tiny green peas add a decorative touch to this dish.

SCOTTISH HADDOCK

Servings	2	4
Setting	+ + +	+ + +
500 watts	min 7	min 12
600/650 watts	$6^{1}/2$	11
700 watts	6	10
Standing Time	4	6
Calories	310	
Fat Content	Very Low (8 g)	
Utensil: Gratin Dish	$1^{1}/2$ qt (1.5 l)	2 qt (2 l)
Ingredients		
Haddock filets	1 lb (450 g)	2 lb (900 g)
Milk	1 cyp	2 cups
Lemon juice	1 tbsp	2 tbsp
Chives or dill	1 tbsp	2 tbsp
Whisky	1 tbsp	2 tbsp
Pepper	1/2 tsp	1 tsp
Salt	1/4 tsp	1/2 tsp

Select an attractive haddock filet.

Blend milk, lemon juice, chives, whisky, salt and pepper.

Lay haddock steaks in mixture.

- Select a nice looking haddock filet.
- Slice into thin steaks.
- Blend milk, lemon juice, chives, whisky, salt and pepper; pour into the dish.
- Arrange haddock steaks in this mixture.
- Cook in microwave according to chart instructions.
- Turn steaks over once during cooking process.
- Enjoy this dish with brandied cherries and candied potatoes. *(see pp. 214 and 215).*

Although haddock has a reputation as an expensive fish, its flavor makes it worth every penny.

STRIPED BASS CHINESE STYLE

Servings	•2•	•4•
Setting	+ + +	+ + +
500 watts	min 9 1/2	min 17
600/650 watts	8 1/2	15
700 watts	8	14
Standing Time	5	7
Calories	310	
Fat Content	Negligeable	
Utensil: Shallow rectangular Dish	12 in × 7*	14 in × 8*
Ingredients		
Whole Striped Bass	1 1/4 lb (550 g)	2 1/2 lbs (1,15 kg)
Medium size orange(s)	1	2
Lemon(s)	1	2
Lime(s)	1	2
Medium size green pepper	1/2	1
Medium size tomatoes	2	4
Medium size onion(s)	1	2
Bean sprouts	1/2 cup	1 cup
Chopped thyme	1 tsp	2 tsp
Chopped mint	1 tsp	2 tsp
Chopped tarragon	1 tsp	2 tsp
Ketchup	2 tbsp	4 tbsp
Tomato juice	1/4 cup	1/2 cup
Vinegar	2 tbsp	4 tbsp
Powdered sugar	2 tbsp	4 tbsp
Soya sauce	2 tbsp	4 tbsp
Tabasco sauce	2 drops	4 drops
Salt	To taste	
Powdered ginger	1/4 tsp	1/2 tsp

* 12 in × 7 = (30 cm × 18)
14 in × 8 = (35 cm × 20)

Have the fish prepared by the fishmonger or do it yourself according to directions on p. 92.

Peel and slice orange, lemon, lime, and onion. Slice tomatoes, dice green pepper.

Set the striped bass in the cooking dish. Cover it with fruit, vegetables and bean sprouts.

Pour sauce over fish. Sprinkle with chopped herbs.

- Ask fishmonger to prepare fish or prepare yourself according to directions on p. 92.
- Peel and cut orange, lemon, lime and onion into very thin slices. Slice the tomatoes unpeeled.
- Chop the herbs, drain bean sprouts and dice the green pepper.
- Lay striped bass in cooking dish. Arrange orange, lemon, lime and onion slices and the chopped tomato, soya sprouts and diced pepper on and around fish.
- For the sauce, blend ketchup, tomato juice, vinegar, powdered sugar, tabasco and soya sauces, ginger. Add salt if necessary (the soya sauce and ketchup are already salty).
- Pour sauce over fish. Sprinkle with chopped herbs.
- Cover with wax paper and cook in microwave according to chart instructions. Turn once during cooking process.
- Serve with French bread.

In minutes, the delicious oriental aroma of this dish will make your mouth water.

TROUT AMANDINE

Servings	1	2
Setting	+ + +	+ + +
500 watts	min 5	min $7^1/_2$
600/650 watts	$4^1/_2$	$6^1/_2$
700 watts	4	6
Standing Time	3	5
Calories	420	
Fat Content	Average (30 g)	
Utensil: Oval Gratin Dish	$^3/_4$ qt (0.75 l)	$1^1/_4$ qt (1.25 l)
Ingredients		
Whole trout	1	2
Medium size red pepper	$^1/_4$	$^1/_2$
Slivered almonds	2 tbsp	4 tbsp
Lime	1	2
Salted butter	1 tsp	2 tsp
Chopped parsley	2 tsp	4 tsp
Pepper	$^1/_4$ tsp	$^1/_2$ tsp
Salt	$^1/_4$ tsp	$^1/_2$ tsp

The success of this recipe depends on the freshness of the trout.

Cut the red pepper into julienne, or thin sticks.

Protect the head and tail of the trout with aluminum foil; remove it halfway through cooking.

- Make sure the trout are cleaned and gutted. Protect head and tail with aluminum foil *(see p. 22)*.
- Slice red pepper into julienne or thin sticks.
- Salt and pepper inside of fish and stuff with lime. This gives a wonderful flavor and keeps the fish moist.
- Set trout in dish. Sprinkle with slivered almonds, chopped parsley, red pepper and small pieces of butter. Add a dash of pepper.
- Cover with wax paper and cook in microwave according to chart directions. Turn fish over halfway through cooking and remove aluminum foil.
- At the end of the standing time, sprinkle the rest of the parsley over the fish and serve at once.

The freshness of the trout determines the flavor of this dish; nothing can beat the taste of freshly caught trout from the nearest stream.

SALMON WITH FRESH HERBS

Servings	• 1 •	2 •
Setting	+ + +	+ + +
500 watts	min 5	min 10
600/650 watts	$4\frac{1}{2}$	9
700 watts	4	8
Standing Time	3	4
Calories	550	
Fat Content	Quite High (45 g)	
Utensil: Rectangular Shallow Dish	8 in × 5* *	8 in × 6* **
Ingredients		
Salmon steaks	1	2
Whipping cream	1/4 cup	1/2 cup
Lemon juice	1/2 tbsp	1 tbsp
Fresh herbs (parsley, chives, tarragon, thyme, etc.)	2 tbsp	4 tbsp
Paprika	1/2 tsp	1 tsp
Pepper	1/4 tsp	1/2 tsp
Salt	1/4 tsp	1/2 tsp

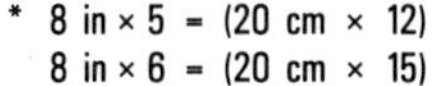
* 8 in × 5 = (20 cm × 12)
8 in × 6 = (20 cm × 15)

Choose a lovely fresh salmon and the freshest herbs.

Arrange the salmon steaks in cooking dish.

Prepare sauce and pour over fish and herbs.

Make sure fish steaks are well bathed in sauce.

- Choose the freshest salmon you can find.
- Cut in 1 in (28 mm) thick steaks.
- Arrange the salmon steaks in the cooking dish.
- Chop the fresh herbs.
- Blend cream, herbs, lemon juice, paprika, salt and pepper.
- Pour over salmon, making sure all of fish is covered.
- Cover dish and cook in microwave according to chart directions. Half way through cooking process, turn fish and recover with sauce.
- Serve at the end of the standing time.

Despite its name, this recipe can also be made with dried herbs, and is especially good with dehydrated herbs (process found on p. 38.)

Fish en Papillote

Servings	4	6
Setting	+ + +	+ + +
500 watts	min 15	min 20
600/650 watts	$13^1/2$	18
700 watts	12	17
Standing Time	5	7
Calories	400 to 450 (depending on kind of fish)	
Fat Content	Low (12 to 19 g)	
Utensil: Wax paper		
Ingredients		
Striped Bass, salmon or other whole fish	2 lbs (900 g)	3 lbs (1.35 kg)
Fennel Bulb(s)	1	2
Medium size tomatoes	2	3
Green pepper	1/2	1
Green onions	8	12
Lime	1	2
Chopped chives	1 tbsp	2 tbsp
Chopped parsley	1 tbsp	2 tbsp
Butter	1/4 cup	1/3 cup
Paprika	2 tsp	3 tsp
Flour	2 tbsp	3 tbsp
Pepper	1 tsp	1 1/2 tsp
Salt	1 tsp	1 1/2 tsp
Oil	A trickle	

*Coat fish with oil.
Sprinkle salt and pepper inside fish.*

Shape a large wax paper wrapper to contain fish.

Combine butter with flour, paprika, salt and pepper.

Spread butter mixture over fish. Fold the paper shut.

- Ask fishmonger to prepare fish or clean yourself as per instructions on p. 92. Coat with small amount of oil; sprinkle insides with salt and pepper.
- Cut fennel into thin slices and tomatoes and lime into rounds; dice the green pepper. Leave onions whole if small; cut larger ones in half.
- Using wax paper, make an envelope large enough to hold the fish.
- Sprinkle fish with fennel, tomatoes, green pepper, onion and lime.
- Add chopped chives and parsley.
- Combine butter with flour, paprika salt and pepper, and work it to a smooth consistency.
- Spread butter mixture over fish. Close the paper over the fish. Cook in microwave according to chart directions. Turn fish over once during cooking process. Let stand before serving.

Open the fish en papilotte at the table so that your guests can enjoy the fragrant aroma escaping.

Halibut New England Style

Servings	1	2
Setting	+ + +	+ + +
500 watts	min $4^1/2$	min $7^1/2$
600/650 watts	4	$6^1/2$
700 watts	$3^1/2$	6
Standing Time	3	4
Calories	300	
Fat Content	Low (15 g)	
Utensil: Cooking Dish	6 in (15 cm)	8 in (20 cm)
Ingredients		
Halibut Steak(s)	1	2
Ketchup	2 tbsp	4 tbsp
White cheese (20% m.g.)	2 tbsp	4 tbsp
Bread crumbs	1 tbsp	2 tbsp
Hot mustard	1 tbsp	2 tbsp
Paprika	1 tsp	2 tsp
Salt	1/8 tsp	1/4 tsp
Tabasco sauce	1 dash	2 dashes
Lemon and chives	(optional)	

Select only the freshest halibut steaks, about 1/2 in (14 mm) thick.

Blend ketchup, white cheese, bread crumbs, mustard, paprika, tabasco sauce and salt.

Spread mixture over halibut steaks. Slice steaks in two for quicker, more even cooking.

Arrange halibut on cooking dish and cover with plastic wrap.

- Choose the freshest halibut steaks, about 1/2 in (14 mm) thick.
- Combine ketchup, white cheese, bread crumbs, hot mustard, paprika, tabasco sauce and salt in the blender.
- Blend mixture until creamy.
- Spread mixture over fish.
- Slice halibut steaks in two lengthwise for faster, more even cooking.
- Put steaks on cooking plate. Cover with plastic wrap with hole cut in center to allow steam to escape. Cook in microwave according to chart directions.
- At the end of standing time, decorate halibut steaks with thin slices lemon and chopped chives.

Halibut is one of the most popular and succulent fish in North America.

Tuna Steaks "Cavalier"

Servings	2	4
Setting	+ + +	+ + +
500 watts	min 10	min *
600/650 watts	9	
700 watts	8	
Standing Time	3	

Calories	500**
Fat Content	Average (35 g)

Utensil: Plate or Browning Dish

Ingredients		
Tuna Steaks approximately 1 in. thick and 1 lb each (28 mm and 450 g)	1	2
Commercial or homemade browning mix *(see p. 30)*	1/4 cup	1/2 cup
Egg(s)	1	2
Pepper	1/2 tsp	1 tsp
Salt	1/2 tsp	1 tsp
Chopped parsley	1 tsp	2 tsp
Tartar sauce (optional)	1/2 cup	1 cup

* Cook in two batches of two servings each.

** Without tartar sauce.

Have the fishmonger prepare large, thick tuna steaks.

Baste with browning sauce. Cook on browning dish.

Turn tuna steak back over and crack an egg on top 3 minutes before end of cooking time.

- Ask the fishmonger to prepare large thick tuna steaks. One steak should be enough to serve two or three.
- Baste tuna steak on both sides with browning sauce.
- Preheat browning plate (*see pages 20 and 21*).
- Set tuna steak on browning plate and push it firmly against the surface to ensure even browning.
- After 1 minute, turn to brown other side.
- Finish cooking process according to chart instructions.
- Three minutes before end of cooking time, turn the steak back over and crack an egg on top. Finish cooking and let stand for 3 minutes.
- Sprinkle with salt, pepper and chopped parsley. Serve plain or with tartar sauce.

Prepared in this fashion, tuna lives up to its reputation as "King of the sea."

SOLE CROQUETTES WITH LUMPFISH CAVIAR

Servings	•2•	•4•
Setting	++	++
500 watts	min 7	min 12
600/650 watts	6	$10^1/_2$
700 watts	5	9
Standing Time	3	5
Calories	430	
Fat Content	Quite Low (21 g)	
Utensil: Ramekin for Sauce and wax paper	Single	Double
Ingredients		
Sole Filets	1/2 lb (225 g)	1 lb (450 g)
Small peeled shrimp	5 oz (140 g)	10 oz (280 g)
Whipping cream	1 tbsp	2 tbsp
Eggs	2	4
Flour	2 tbsp	4 tbsp
Light cream	1/4 cup	1/2 cup
Red lumpfish caviar	2 tbsp	4 tbsp
Pepper	1/2 tsp	1 tsp
Salt	1/4 tsp	1/2 tsp

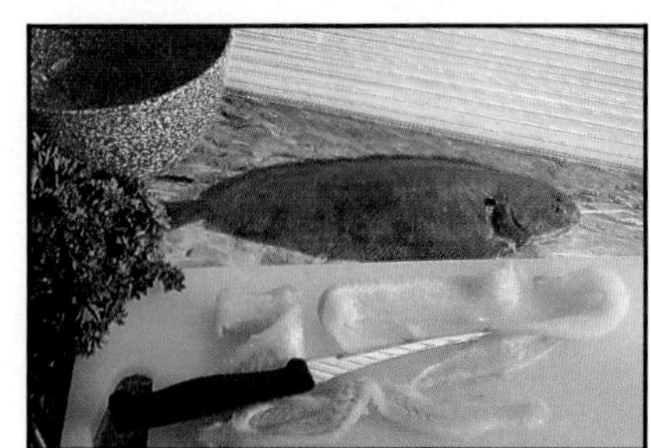

Choose the freshest sole filets. If using frozen, defrost according to direction on p. 24.

Drain shrimp. Separate the eggs.

Blend the sole and shrimp with whipping cream. Add egg yolk and flour mixture and whipped egg whites.

Shape the mixture into croquettes and set on wax paper.

- Choose the freshest filets of sole. If using frozen fish, defrost according to directions on p. 24.
- Coarsely chop the sole and put in blender with well-drained shrimp and whipping cream. Blend till smooth.
- Separate the eggs.
- Beat egg yolks with flour and add to fish mixture.
- Whip egg whites until thick and foamy; incorporate into fish mixture.
- Add salt and pepper. Set aside.
- In the ramekin prepare sauce by gently mixing light cream with lumpfish caviar.
- Shape fish mixture into croquettes with a spoon.
- Set croquettes on wax paper.
- Cook in microwave according to chart directions.
- Halfway through cooking process, cover croquettes with wax paper and put sauce in oven alongside. Finish cooking. Let stand. Pour the caviar mixture over the croquettes. Serve immediately.

This sophisticated gourmet dish can be prepared in a snap.

Breaded Fish in Tomatoes

Servings	1	2
Setting	+ +	+ +
	min	min
500 watts	4	6
600/650 watts	3 3/4	5 1/2
700 watts	3 1/2	5
Standing Time	3	4
Calories	290	
Fat Content	Low (18 g)	
Utensil: Rectangular gratin dish	3/4 qt (0.75 l)	1 1/2 qt (1.5 l)
Ingredients		
Fish filets, thawed	2	4
Eggs	1	2
Tomato pulp	2 tbsp	4 tbsp
Chopped parsley	2 tbsp	4 tbsp
Cayenne pepper	1/8 tsp	1/4 tsp
Salt	1/4 tsp	1/2 tsp
Tomato sauce	To garnish	

Separate the eggs.
Finely chop the parsley.

Whip egg whites into stiff peaks.
Beat in tomato pulp.

Arrange breaded fish filets in gratin dish.
Sprinkle generously with parsley
and pour egg mixture over all.

- Separate the eggs.
- Finely chop parsley.
- Whip egg whites into stiff peaks.
- Beat tomato pulp into eggs whites.
- Blend in lightly beaten egg yolks.
- Add cayenne pepper and salt, mix well.
- Arrange breaded fish filets in gratin dish.
- Sprinkle generously with chopped parsley.
- Pour egg mixture on top.
- Cover with wax paper and cook in microwave according to chart instructions.
- Do not turn filets over during cooking; this would disturb the texture and appearance of the egg mixture, which should look like a light tomato omelet.
- Let stand and serve with a tomato sauce.

An elegant way to liven up an everyday food.

SEAFOOD RILLETTES

Servings	•2/3	• 4/5•
Setting	+ + +	+ + +
500 watts	min 5	min 7
600/650 watts	$4^1/_2$	$6^1/_2$
700 watts	4	6
Standing Time	Until dish is cool	
Calories	210	
Fat Content	Low (14 g)	
Utensil: Pyrex Gratin Dish	$1^1/_4$ qt (1.25 l)	2 qt (2 l)
Ingredients		
Haddock filets	$^1/_2$ lb (225 g)	1 lb (450 g)
Crab meat	5 oz (140 g)	10 oz (280 g)
Anchovy filets	$^1/_2$ can	1 can
Butter	2 tbsp	4 tbsp
Chopped parsley	2 tbsp	4 tbsp
Pepper	$^1/_2$ tsp	1 tsp
Salt	To Taste	
Toasted rye bread	To garnish	
Lime	To garnish	

Chunk haddock filets; break up crabmeat; mash anchovy filets with butter.

Grind all fish ingredients in blender to coarse consistency.

Spread the mixture in a gratin dish.

- Cut haddock filets into chunks.
- Break up the crabmeat.
- Mash the anchovy filets with butter.
- Put haddock, crab, anchovies and butter into blender. Add generous amount of pepper and chopped parsley. Process just until coarse; you do not want a smooth paste.
- Taste and add salt to taste (anchovies may be very salty).
- Spread the mixture in a gratin dish.
- Cover with wax paper and cook in microwave according to chart instructions.
- Stir often during cooking process.
- Chill and serve with toasted rye bread.
- Sprinkle with lime juice to taste.

This makes a savory and original main course, entrée or snack, which can be stored two or three days in the refrigerator.

Seafood spaghetti

Servings	2	4
Setting	++	++
500 watts	min 5	min 9
600/650 watts	4 1/2	8
700 watts	4	7
Standing Time	3	4

Calories	340
Fat Content	Negligeable

Utensil: Dish for Scallops and 2 bowls

Ingredients		
Fresh or defrosted Scallops	1/2 lb (225 g)	1 lb (450 g)
Peas	1/3 cup	2/3 cup
Cooked spaghetti	12 oz (350 g)	1 1/2 lbs (675 g)
Small peeled shrimp	1/3 cup	2/3 cup
Tomato pulp	1/2 cup	1 cup
Chopped parsley	1 tbsp	2 tbsp
Pepper	1/4 tsp	1/2 tsp
Salt	1/4 tsp	1/2 tsp

Cook spaghetti according to instructions on p. 37 or chart on p. 197.

Arrange scallops on microwave-safe plate. Cover with wax paper.

Put tomato pulp, shrimp, chopped parsley, salt and pepper in a bowl.

- Cook spaghetti according to instructions on p. 37 or as per chart instructions on p. 197. Keep warm.
- Arrange scallops on plate and cover with wax paper.
- Put peas in a bowl.
- Put the tomato pulp in second bowl; add shrimp, chopped parsley, salt and pepper.
- In microwave, cook scallops, peas and tomato mixture according to chart instructions.
- Half way through cooking process turn scallops; stir peas and tomato pulp.
- At the end of the cooking process, mix scallops and peas into spaghetti. Stir.
- Let stand. Add tomato mixture. Stir and serve immediately.

This dish is just as delicious served cold. Simply add a little olive oil and lemon juice and present as a salad.

Oysters au Gratin

Servings	• 1 •	2 •
Setting	+ + +	+ + +
500 watts	min 4	min 6
600/650 watts	3 1/2	5
700 watts	3	4 1/2
Standing Time	2	3
Calories	300	
Fat Content	Quite Low (20 g)	
Utensil: Round Gratin Dish	6 in (15 cm)	8 in (20 cm)
Ingredients		
Oysters	6	12
Sour cream	1/4 cup	1/2 cup
Lime juice	1 tsp	2 tsp
Baby clams drained	1/4 cup	1/2 cup
Chopped parsley	1 tsp	2 tsp
Paprika	1/2 tsp	1 tsp
Pepper	1/4 tsp	1/2 tsp
Salt	To taste	
Cracker crumbs	2 tbsp	4 tbsp

Pry open oysters.

Drain and filter oyster juice.

Add sour cream, lime juice, chopped parsley, paprika and pepper to filtered oyster juice. Crush crackers.

Add crackers, baby clams and oysters to sour cream mixture. Stir before pouring into baking dish.

- Open oysters if fresh; if frozen, thaw according to chart instructions on p. 24. You can also use canned oysters.
- Drain oysters. Filter oyster liquid thoroughly to remove sand and shell pieces.
- Add sour cream, lime juice, chopped parsley, paprika and pepper to filtered oyster juice.
- Crush crackers and add to sour cream mixture.
- Mix in the baby clams.
- Taste and add salt, if necessary.
- Pour into cooking dish. Spread oysters evenly in dish and cook in microwave according to chart instructions. Stir once during cooking process.
- Let stand and serve while still hot.

Even those who normally shy away from oysters will enjoy this refined gratin dish.

Clams Japanese Style

Servings	1	2
Setting	+ + +	+ + +
500 watts	min 4 + 1	min 6 + 1 1/2
600/650 watts	3 + 1	5 + 1 1/2
700 watts	3 + 1	5 + 1 1/2
Standing Time	2	3
Calories	150	
Fat Content	Very Low (8 g)	
Utensil: Gratin Dish or Plate	6 in (15 cm)	8 in (20 cm)
Ingredients		
Large clams	3	6
Butter	1 tbsp	2 tbsp
Soya sauce	1 tbsp	2 tbsp
Lemon juice	1 tsp	2 tsp
Powdered ginger	1/2 tsp	1 tsp

Arrange clams in a circle in gratin dish.

Clams will open in a few minutes. Discard the unopened ones.

Pull out the top vein. Detach meat of the clam from lower shell with a sharp knife.

Pour sauce over each clam and return to oven.

- Arrange clams in a circle in gratin plate or dish.
- Cook in microwave according to chart instructions.
- At the end of the first cooking time, discard any clams that remain closed; they are probably bad.
- Meanwhile, prepare sauce. Blend butter, soya sauce, lemon juice and powdered ginger.
- Pull out the top vein of the opened clams and detach the clam meat from the shell with a sharp knife.
- Pour sauce over each clam and cook in microwave for second time period on the chart.
- Serve immediately after standing time with French bread.

The Japanese usually serve elegantly small portions, but North Americans can easily devour six clams in one sitting. Do not hesitate to double the portions but do not tell your Japanese friends; They might take you for a glutton!

California Shrimp

Servings	2	4
Setting	+ +	+ +
	min	min
500 watts	6 1/2	*
600/650 watts	6	*
700 watts	5 1/2	*
Standing Time	3	3
Calories	440	
Fat Content	Very Low (8 g)	
Utensil: Double Ramekin	1	2
Ingredients		
Large peeled shrimp	12 oz (340 g)	1 1/2 lbs (675 g)
Corn niblets	1 cup	2 cups
Small peas	1/2 cup	1 cup
Pineapple slices	2	4
Canned red kidney beans	1/2 cup	1 cup
Red pepper	1/2	1
Orange juice	2 tbsp	4 tbsp
Lemon juice	1 tbsp	2 tbsp
Butter	1 tbsp	2 tbsp
Tabasco sauce	3 drops	6 drops
Salt	1/4 tsp	1/2 tsp

* Cook one dish on top shelf, the other on bottom shelf; exchange position half way through cooking process. Add 2 minutes cooking time.

Carefully drain corn niblets, peast and red kidney beans. Dry shrimp on light cloth. Cut pineapple and green pepper into small pieces.

Distribute ingredients into ramekins.

Add butter, lemon and orange juice mixture, salt and tabasco sauce to ingredients.

- Thoroughly drain corn niblets, peas and kidney beans.
- Pat the shrimp dry with paper towel or cloth.
- Cut the pineapple and red pepper into cubes.
- Arrange corn niblets in bottom of ramekins. Add shrimp, red pepper, pineapple, peas and kidney beans.
- Blend lemon juice with orange juice, salt and tabasco sauce. Pour over mixture.
- Top with butter. Cover with wax paper.
- Cook in microwave according to chart instructions. Stir twice during cooking process.
- Let stand before serving.

In this recipe the red peppers are still tender-crisp, as in Chinese cooking. If you prefer, precook them with a spoonful of hot water for 3 minutes on HIGH.

Bar Harbor Lobster

Servings	•2•	•4•
Setting	+++	+++
500 watts	min 12	min *
600/650 watts	11	*
700 watts	10	*
Standing Time	5	

Calories	300	
Fat Content	Quite Low (23 g)	
Utensil: Square Gratin Dish and Bowl	10 in × 10** 1 qt (1 l)	
Ingredients		
Live Lobster*** 2 lbs (900 g) each	1	2
Chopped shallots	2 tbsp	4 tbsp
Chopped garlic	1 tsp	2 tsp
Chopped parsley	1 tbsp	2 tbsp
Chopped tarragon	1 tbsp	2 tbsp
Whipping cream	2 tbsp	4 tbsp
Tomato juice	1/2 cup	1 cup
Lemon juice	1 tbsp	2 tbsp
Dry white wine	2 tbsp	4 tbsp
Butter	2 tbsp	4 tbsp
Cayenne pepper	1/4 tsp	1/2 tsp
Paprika	1 tsp	2 tsp
Salt	1/4 tsp	1/2 tsp

* Cook in two stages of two servings each.
** 10 in × 10 = 25 cm × 25

*** In France, it is traditional to cut up the lobster while it is still alive. It may be the purists' approach but nowadays, it seems cruel. You can boil the lobster in a court-bouillon before cutting or simply defrost and cup up a frozen lobster.

Cut up lobster.

Gather up shell juice and creamy substance in shell. Prepare all ingredients for sauce.

Arrange lobster pieces in gratin dish. Pour sauce into cooking bowl.

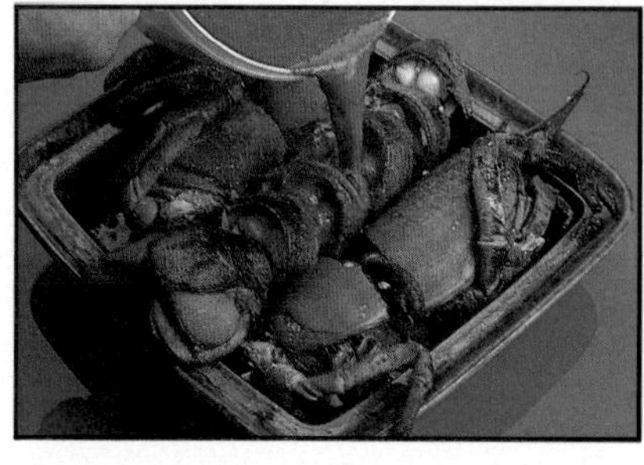

Half way through cooking process, run sauce through blender and pour over lobster.

- Cut up lobster. Save the lobster juice and creamy drippings. Keep claws for another recipe (*See CLAWS COCO on pages 130 and 131*).
- Blend all ingredients for the sauce: chopped shallots, garlic, parsley, cream, tomato juice, lemon juice, white wine, cayenne pepper, paprika and salt.
- Mash the butter with creamy substance from lobster.
- Add butter mixture and reserved lobster juice to sauce ingredients. Stir.
- Arrange lobster pieces in ramekin dish. Pour sauce into bowl and cook both dishes in microwave according to chart instructions..
- Half way through cooking time, run the sauce through blender. Turn lobster over and cover with sauce.
- Return to oven and finish cooking.
- Serve immediately after standing time is complete.

For an original and sophisticated presentation, you can empty the lobster tail and arrange as illustrated, decorated with the tail tip and legs and an herb bouquet to represent the lobster head.

LOBSTER BROCHETTES WITH LIME

Servings	1	2
Setting	+ + +	+ + +
	min	min
500 watts	3	6
600/650 watts	$2\frac{3}{4}$	$5\frac{1}{2}$
700 watts	$2\frac{1}{2}$	5
Standing Time	2	3
Calories	280	
Fat Content	Low (12 g)	
Utensil: Plate	8 in (20 cm)	10 in (25 cm)
Ingredients		
Raw Lobster Tail(s)* 10 oz (280 g) each	1	2
Lime(s)	1	2
Olive oil	1 tbsp	2 tbsp
Chopped chives	1 tsp	2 tsp
Pepper	$\frac{1}{4}$ tsp	$\frac{1}{2}$ tsp
Salt	$\frac{1}{4}$ tsp	$\frac{1}{2}$ tsp

* or lightly cooked in court-bouillon to facilitate shelling.

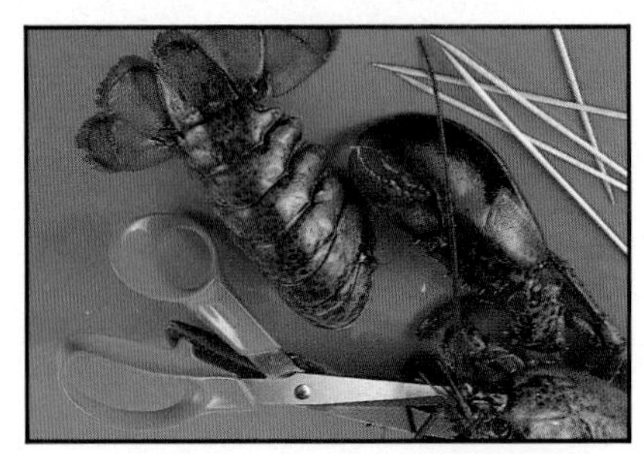

Preferably use fresh lobster tails.

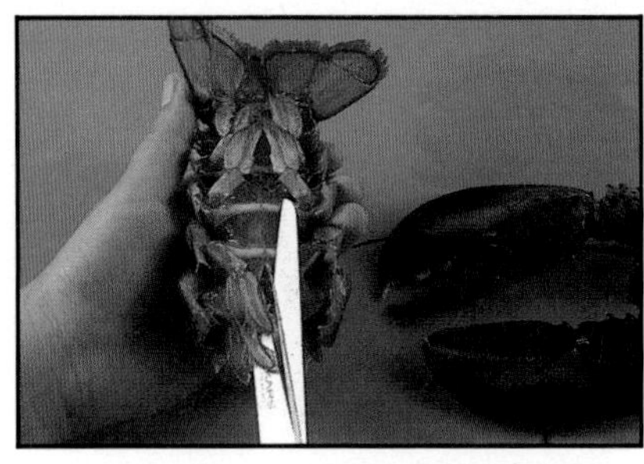

Using scissors, cut through cartilage on underside of tail; shell tails.

Slice tail into medallions and slip onto wooden skewers, separating each with a slice of lime.

- Preferably use fresh lobster tails. If frozen, make sure they are completely thawed.
- With scissors, cut through cartilage on underside of tail. Carefully peel off the rings of shell, being careful to keep the lobster meat in one piece.
- Slice tail crosswise into medallions.
- Slide medallions onto wooden skewers, with a slice of lime separating each medallion.
- Cover with wax paper and cook in microwave according to chart instructions.
- Half way through cooking process, turn brochettes. Add salt and pepper to taste and a bit of olive oil.
- Cover once again with wax paper and complete cooking process.
- Let stand; sprinkle with chopped chives and serve.

This delicacy is equally good served cold garnished with a tossed green salad.

Lobster au gratin

Servings	2	4
Setting	+ +	+ +
500 watts	min 5	min 7
600/650 watts	4 1/2	6 1/2
700 watts	4	6
Standing Time	2	3
Calories	440	
Fat Content	Quite low (27 g)	
Utensil: round gratin dish	8 in (20 cm)	10 in (25 cm)
Ingredients		
Lobster, 1 lb (450 g) each, cooked in court-bouillon	2	4
Whipping cream	1/2 cup	1 cup
Tomato paste	1 tbsp	2 tbsp
Powdered saffron	1/4 tsp	1/2 tsp
Pepper	1/4 tsp	1/2 tsp
Salt	1/4 tsp	1/2 tsp
Chopped parsley	1 tbsp	2 tbsp
Chopped thyme	1 tsp	2 tsp
Grated gruyère	1 tbsp	2 tbsp

Shell cooked lobster tails.

Slice tails into medallions, arrange in gratin dish and cover with sauce.

Sprinkle with grated gruyère, chopped parsley and chopped thyme.

- Shell lobster tails as explained in previous recipe.
- Remove creamy substance from shells. Set aside claws and legs for another recipe.
- Slice lobster tails into medallions. Arrange them in gratin dish.
- Blend together cream, tomato paste, the creamy lobster substance, saffron, salt and pepper.
- Spread this sauce mixture over medallions.
- Sprinkle with grated gruyère, chopped parsley and thyme.
- Cover with wax paper and cook in microwave according to chart instructions.
- Stir twice during cooking process.
- Let stand then serve immediately as is or with Indian rice.

This is definitely one of the finest dishes in the history of gastronomy.

Lobster claws coco

Servings	• 1 •	2 •
Setting	+ + +	+ + +
500 watts	min + 2*	min + 2*
600/650 watts	+ 2*	+ 3*
700 watts	+ 2*	+ 3*
Standing Time	+ 3*	+ 3*
Calories	460	
Fat Content	Average (36 g)	
Utensil: Pyrex Casserole	1/2 qt (0.5 l)	1 qt (1 l)
Ingredients		
Large lobster claw(s)	1	2
Egg(s)	1	2
Paprika	1 tsp	2 tsp
Pepper	1/2 tsp	1 tsp
Salt	1/2 tsp	1 tsp
Grated coconut	1/2 cup	1 cup
Curry powder	1/2 tsp	1 tsp
Oil for frying	1 cup	2 cups
Bearnaise or Cocktail sauce	As garnish	

* Figure on 5 to 8 minutes for the oil to come to a boil.

Shell lobster claws.

Beat eggs, paprika, salt and pepper.

Dip lobster claws into egg mixture.

Coat lobster claws with coconut. Sprinkle with curry.

- Shell lobster claws. You will have an easier time of it if you first immerse claws in boiling water for a few minutes.
- Beat eggs, paprika, salt and pepper.
- Pour oil into casserole and cook in microwave until oil begins to boil.
- Meanwhile, dip each lobster claw in egg mixture, then roll lobster claw in grated coconut.
- Sprinkle with curry powder.
- When oil begins to sizzle, drop claws into it.
- Cook according to chart instructions.
- Turn claws over half way through cooking process.
- Let stand on paper towels, then serve with cocktail sauce or cold bearnaise sauce.

An exquisite way to discover the versatility of coconut.

Broiled Lobster

Servings	2	4
Setting	+ + +	+ + +
500 watts	min 5	min 8
600/650 watts	$4^1/2$	7
700 watts	4	6
Standing Time	3	5
Calories	220	
Fat Content	Very Low (7 g)	
Utensil: Oval Gratin Dish	1 qt (1 l)	2 qt (2 l)
Ingredients		
Live Lobster* (approx 2 lbs) (900 g)	1	2
Whipping cream	2 tbsp	4 tbsp
Chopped shallots	1 tbsp	2 tbsp
Chopped chervil	1 tbsp	2 tbsp
Pepper	1/2 tsp	1 tsp
Salt	1/4 tsp	1/2 tsp

* See note on p. 124

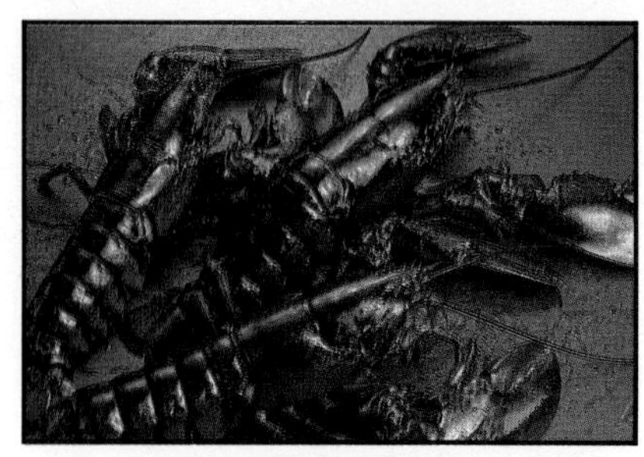

Select fresh, healthy lobster of the same size.

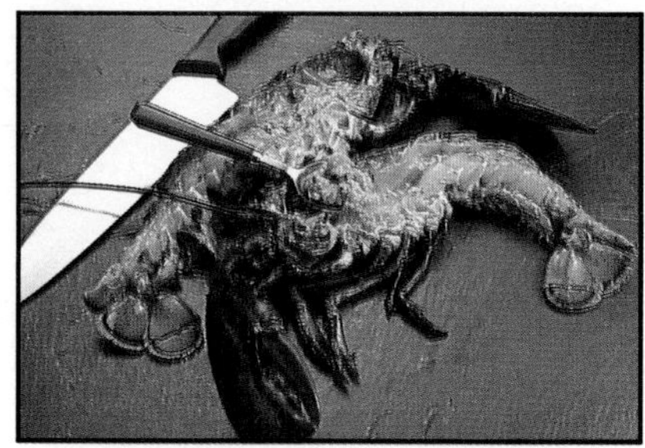

Split the lobster in two, lengthwise. Set aside the creamy substance.

Break the claws to cook more rapidly.

Arrange the halved lobster in the gratin dish. Pour the sauce over the lobster meat.

- It is essential to select fresh, healthy lobster. When preparing two, make sure they are the same size so that cooking time is the same.
- Split lobster in two, lengthwise.
- Collect the juice and the creamy substance from the shell.
- Break open the claws, but leave them attached to the body.
- Combine lobster juice and creamy substance, whipping cream, finely chopped shallots, chopped chervil, salt and pepper. Mix with a fork to a thick, creamy texture.
- Arrange lobster halves, shell side down, in the gratin dish.
- Pour cream mixture over lobster meat. Cover with plastic wrap; cut hole in top to allow steam to escape. Cook in the microwave according to chart instructions.
- Let stand and serve.

The shell of lobster broiled in the microwave does not turn the familiar "lobster red" color, but the meat is just as tasty and juicy.

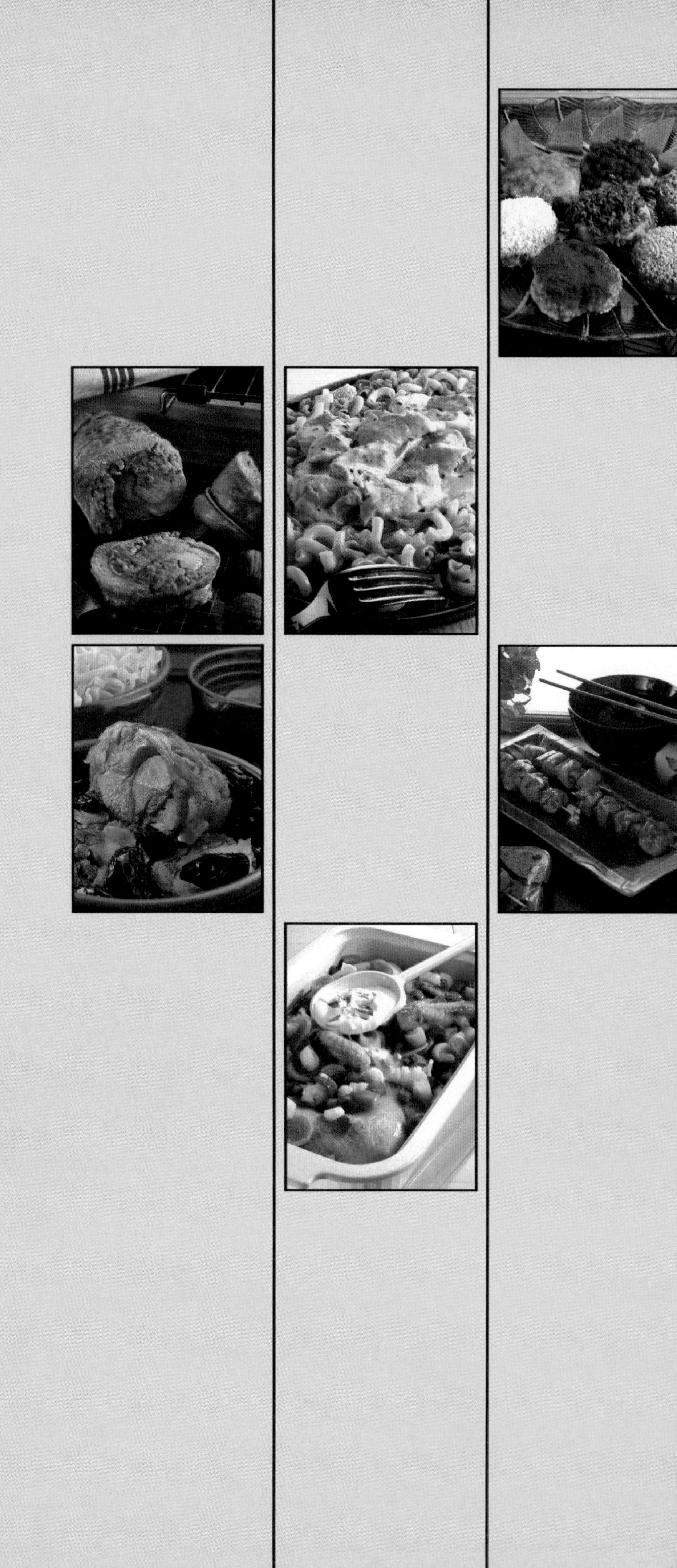

POULTRY

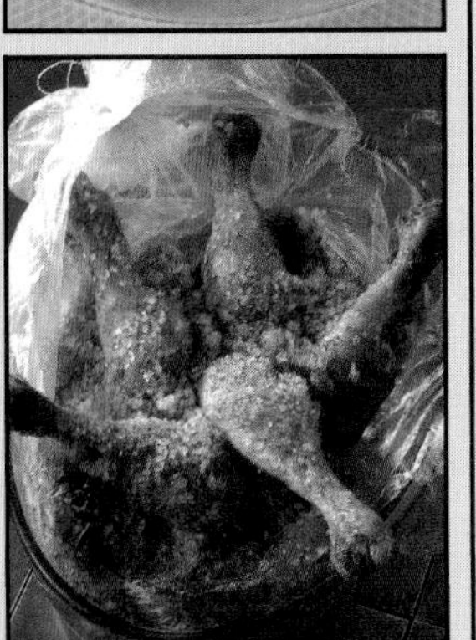

COOKING CHART

FOOD	WEIGHT	COOKING TIME (MIN) 500W	600/650W	700W	SETTING
Chicken, cut up	1 lb (450 g)	7 min	6½ min	6 min	+ + +
Chicken, whole	3 lb (1.5 kg)	28 min	26 min	24 min	+ + +
Duck, 2 breasts, pink	1 lb (450 g)	5 min	4½ min	4 min	+ + +
well done	1 lb (450 g)	7 min	6½ min	6 min	+ + +
Duck, whole	4½ lb (2 kg)	20 min	18½ min	17 min	+ + +
Quail, 3 birds	1 lb (450 g)	8 min	7½ min	7 min	+ + + plus + +
Quail, 6 birds	2 lb (900 g)	13 min	12 min	11 min	+ + + plus + +
Turkey, leg or quarter	per 1 lb (450 g)	10 min	9½ min	9 min	+ + +
Turkey, whole	per 1 lb (450 g)	16 min	15½ min	14 min	+ +

Turn poultry or poultry pieces a number of times during cooking. To brown poultry, you can use a browning plate and browning mix, as well as glazes (*see pages 20, 21, 32, 33 and 34*).

In general, poultry is better if cut up and cooked in the microwave at maximum power. Whole birds weighing more than 3 lbs (1.5 kg) should be cooked at 70% power or MEDIUM HIGH. Large birds, such as capons, turkey and geese, should be cooked slowly at 50% power, or MEDIUM.

Stuffing and Rolling Poultry or Meat

Stuffed poultry or meat is as spectacular as it is delicious. And since microwave ovens lend themselves particularly well to this type of cuisine, we have presented several recipes of this style.

The first step, however, is to master the art of boning, rolling and tying.

Boning is not always necessary for rolled roasts; for example, you can often start with a boneless cut. However, with turkey for example, many people prefer the taste and texture of the leg (which has a bone) to the boneless breast. So why not offer a rolled drumstick?

Is it Difficult to Debone a Turkey Leg?

No, all you need is a cutting board and a good sharp knife. Proceed as follows:

Cut through the flesh along the side of the bone. Continue to cut along the bone with small cuts until it is completely detached from the flesh. Be careful not to cut through the skin; you will have trouble rolling it.

Once the bone is removed, pull out the nerves and large fibers or pieces of fat. If the piece is too irregular in thickness, trim it with a knife; you can use the trimmings in the stuffing.

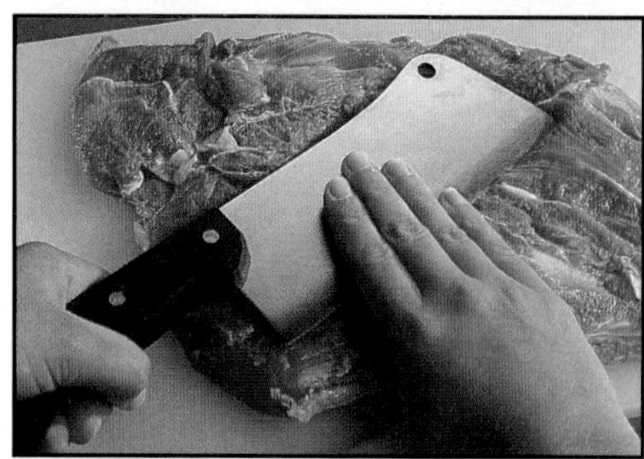

Pound the flesh with a kitchen mallet or the side of a cleaver to make thinner and more even. The flesh will be easier to roll and more tender.

How Do You Tie a Rolled Piece of Meat or a Roast?

It's easy. But for the moment, let's forget the turkey drumstick and look at a piece of red meat, so that the string is easier to see.

No matter what king of stuffing you use, you have to roll the meat with two hands. Use the palms of your hands to hold the rolled part, applying even pressure, and use your fingertips to guide the rolling of the meat, just as you would roll a piece of paper.

Slide the kitchen string under one end of the meat and tie the first knot; never start in the middle or the stuffing can only escape from one end; you can easily contain it with your hand.

Cut the string above the knot, and slide the string under the meat again. Make a second tie about 1/2 in (14 mm) from the first.

Continue tying along the length of the roast in the same way. You only have to trim the ends of the roast even, and the roll is ready to cook.

Won't the Stuffing Full Out During Cooking?

At the beginning, yes, a little. But once the rolled roast has been in the oven for a few minutes, the stuffing will solidify. To eliminate any inconvenience, put the rolled roast in a cooking bag for the first half of cooking time; remove it to finish cooking.

TURKEY DRUMSTICK ROLL

Servings	• 5/7 •
Setting	+ + +
	min
500 watts	20
600/650 watts	18 1/2
700 watts	17
Standing Time	7
Calories	450
Fat Content	Average (32 g)

Utensil: Dish with steamer or *trivet* (*see p. 19*)

Ingredients	
Turkey Leg approx. 2 lbs (1 kg)	1
Yogurt	Single Serving
Plain chestnuts	1 cup
Sausage meat	1/4 lb (120 g)
Chopped onion	1/4 cup
Chopped parsley	2 tbsp
Hot mustard	2 tbsp
Pepper	1/2 tsp
Salt	1/2 tsp
Browning mixture (*see p. 30*)	1/2 cup

Bone the turkey leg as explained on p. 136.

Blend yogurt, chestnuts, sausage meat, onion, parsley, mustard, salt and pepper in blender.

Lay boned turkey leg flat, skin side down, and spread stuffing evenly on top.

Roll and tie as shown on p. 137. Baste with browning mixture.

- Ask the butcher to bone the turkey leg or bone it yourself; (see directions on p. 136.)
- Put yogurt, chestnuts, sausage meat, onion, parsley, mustard, salt and pepper into blender. Add any scraps of turkey meat from the boning process.
- Process to a smooth texture.
- Lay the boned turkey leg flat, skin side down. Spread stuffing evenly over meat.
- Roll and tie as shown on p. 137.
- Baste rolled drumstick with browning mixture and cook in the microwave as per chart instructions.
- Let stand before carving. Serve hot, or cold for a picnic or buffet table.

An extraordinary and most succulent dish. Haute cuisine at its best, yet simple to prepare!

ROAST TURKEY WITH PRUNES

Servings	•2/3 •	4/5•
Setting	+ + +	+ + +
500 watts	min 10	min 19
600/650 watts	$9^1/_2$	18
700 watts	9	17
Standing Time	7	9
Calories	580	
Fat Content	Average (30 g)	
Utensil: Shallow Round Dish	8 in (20 cm)	10 in (25 cm)
Ingredients		
Turkey roast	1 lb (450 g)	2 lbs (900 g)
Prunes	1/2 lb (225 g)	1 lb (450 g)
Red wine	1/2 cup	1 cup
Honey	3 tbsp	4 tbsp
Vinegar	1 tbsp	2 tbsp
Pepper	1/2 tsp	1 tsp
Salt	1/3 tsp	2/3 tsp
Paprika	1 tsp	2 tsp

Pit prunes and soak in red wine for 1 hour.

Dilute honey in vinegar.

Baste turkey with honey-vinegar mixture.

Season wine with salt and pepper; arrange marinated prunes around turkey and pour seasoned wine over meat. Sprinkle turkey with paprika before cooking in microwave.

- Pit prunes and let soak in red wine for at least 1 hour.
- Dissolve the honey in vinegar.
- Set turkey roast in dish and baste heavily with honey vinegar mixture.
- Season wine-soaked prunes with salt and pepper.
- Arrange prunes around roast.
- Pour wine and the rest of honey-vinegar over turkey.
- Sprinkle paprika over turkey and cook in microwave according to chart instructions.
- Baste often during cooking.
- Half way through process, turn over turkey and stir prunes.
- Let stand before serving. Serve with fresh pasta.

A good old-fashioned dish with a flavor that will please the whole family!

TURKEY SCALOPPINI ITALIAN

Servings	•2/3	• 4/5•
Setting	+ + +	+ + +
500 watts	min 5	min 8
600/650 watts	$4^1/_2$	$7^1/_2$
700 watts	4	7
Standing Time	2	3
Calories	410	
Fat Content	Average (30 g)	
Utensil: Oval Gratin Dish	1 qt (1 l)	$1^1/_2$ qt (1.5 l)
Ingredients		
Turkey filets	1 lb (450 g)	2 lbs (900 g)
Light table cream (10% m.g.)	$^1/_2$ cup	1 cup
Lemon juice	1 tbsp	2 tbsp
Marsala or Port wine	2 tbsp	4 tbsp
Worcestershire sauce	$^1/_2$ tsp	1 tsp
Chopped chives	1 tbsp	2 tbsp
Curry powder	$^1/_2$ tsp	1 tsp
Pepper	$^1/_4$ tsp	$^1/_2$ tsp
Salt	$^1/_4$ tsp	$^1/_2$ tsp
Egg Noodles	As side dish	

Slice turkey filets into thin escalopes.

Prepare sauce: combine well the light cream, lemon juice, Marsala or Port, Worcestershire sauce, chopped chives, curry, salt and pepper.

Coat bottom of dish with a layer of sauce, spread turkey escalopes on top. Repeat procedure until all ingredients are used.

- Slice turkey filets into thin escalopes, called "saltimbocca" in Italian cuisine.
- Cook noodles as described on p. 37 and chart directions on p. 197. Keep warm.
- Prepare sauce: Combine light cream, lemon juice, Marsala or Port, Worcestershire sauce, chopped chives, curry, salt and pepper.
- Coat bottom of cooking dish with a layer of sauce, lay turkey on top. Repeat, alternating layers until all ingredients are used.
- Cover dish and cook in microwave according to chart directions.
- Half way through cooking process, stir ingredients from the edge to the center of dish, and scoop them from bottom to top.
- Serve with egg noodles.

You can liven up this Italian meal even more by serving noodles in assorted colors.

Chicken Blanquette

Servings	•4/5	• 8/9•
Setting	+ + +	+ + +
	min	min
500 watts	17	30
600/650 watts	16	28
700 watts	15	26
Standing Time	5	8
Calories	420	
Fat Content	Quite Low (28 g)	
Utensil: Shallow rectangular dish	$1^1/2$ qt (1.5 l)	$2^1/2$ qt (2.5 l)
Ingredients		
Chicken, average weight	1	2
Carrots	1/2 lb (225 g)	1 lb (450 g)
Leek, medium size	1	2
Minced onion	1/4 cup	1/2 cup
Green pepper, medium size	1/2	1
Cauliflower or broccoli	1/2 lb (225 g)	1 lb (450 g)
Chopped tarragon	1 tbsp	2 tbsp
Lemon juice	1 tbsp	2 tbsp
Whipping cream	1/2 cup	1 cup
Chicken stock (preferably warm)	1 cup	2 cups
Pepper	1 tsp	2 tsp
Salt	1 tsp	2 tsp

Select a fresh, lean chicken of average size. Wash vegetables.

Cut up chicken and chop vegetables.

Arrange chicken and vegetables in cooking dish. Pour chicken stock over all ingredients.

- Select a lean fresh chicken of average size; choose fresh vegetables.
- Wash vegetables. Slice carrots and leek into thin rings, chop green pepper into cubes and break up cauliflower into flowerets. Mince onion, or use whole small new onions.
- Cut chicken into pieces.
- Arrange chicken pieces on cooking dish and add vegetables.
- Sprinkle chicken stock with salt and pepper and pour over all ingredients in dish. (It is best to preheat the stock).
- Cover and cook in microwave according to chart instructions.
- Half way through cooking process, turn chicken pieces and gently stir vegetables. Add lemon juice.
- Five minutes before end of cooking process, pour cream over all ingredients and sprinkle with chopped tarragon. Stir to blend and finish cooking.

This chicken blanquette is low in cost but high in taste and appeal.

POULTRY MEDALLIONS

Servings	•2/3	• 4/6•
Setting	+ + +	+ + +
500 watts	min 3	min *
600/650 watts	$2^{3}/_{4}$	*
700 watts	$2^{2}/_{3}$	*
Standing Time	3	
Calories	490	
Fat Content	Quite High (41 g)	
Utensil: Use Wax Paper		
Ingredients		
Chicken filets	$^{1}/_{4}$ lb (115 g)	$^{1}/_{2}$ lb (230 g)
Duck filets	$^{1}/_{4}$ lb (115 g)	$^{1}/_{2}$ lb (230 g)
Sausage meat	$^{1}/_{4}$ lb (115 g)	$^{1}/_{2}$ lb (230 g)
Egg(s)	1	2
Flour	1 tbsp	2 tbsp
Bread crumbs soaked in milk	$^{1}/_{4}$ cup	$^{1}/_{2}$ cup
Pepper	$^{1}/_{4}$ tsp	$^{1}/_{2}$ tsp
Salt	$^{1}/_{4}$ tsp	$^{1}/_{2}$ tsp
Chopped peanuts or grated coconut	1 tbsp	2 tbsp
Sesame seeds	1 tbsp	2 tbsp
Cranberries	1 tbsp	2 tbsp
Pineapple jam	1 tbsp	2 tbsp
Chopped parsley	1 tbsp	2 tbsp
Paprika	1 tbsp	2 tbsp

* Cook in two batches.

Prepare mixture and garnishes for medallions.

Shape medallions, each weighing approximately 3 oz (85 g).

Roll medallions in one of the following: chopped peanuts or grated coconut, sesame seeds, chopped cranberries, pineapple jam, chopped parsley, paprika...

- Prepare ingredients for poultry medallions: In blender, grind chicken and duck filets along with sausage meat, milk-soaked bread crumbs, flour, salt and pepper.
- Add eggs and blend.
- Shape medallions. They should weigh approximately 3 oz (85 g) each. Prepare 6 for two or three people, 12 for 4 to 6 people.
- Chop peanuts and parsley.
- Roll each medallion in one of the following garnishes: chopped peanuts or grated coconut, sesame seeds, chopped cranberries, pineapple jam, chopped parsley, paprika. The list goes on... allow your imagination to run wild!
- Set each medallion on wax paper directly on the microwave oven floor. Cook no more than 6 medallions at one time. Cover with a second sheet of wax paper.
- Cook in microwave according to chart instructions. Turn over half way through cooking process. Let stand before serving.

This is an unusual and amusing dish with a variety of flavors. It is usually served with slices of watermelon.

YAKITORI

Servings	2	4
Setting	+ + +	+ + +
	min	min
500 watts	6	10
600/650 watts	$5^1/_2$	9
700 watts	5	8
Standing Time	5	7

Calories	200
Fat Content	Very Low (7 g)

Utensil: Browning Dish or Plate
(*See pp. 20, 21*)

Ingredients*		
Chicken filets	1/2 lb (225 g)	1 lb (450 g)
Small leeks	2	4
Teriyaki sauce**	1/2 cup	1 cup
Sansho Japanese spice	2 tsp	4 tsp

* This recipe can easily be doubled.

** If Teriyaki sauce is not available, prepare your own by mixing one part Soya sauce and one part molasses (or caramel); add the juice of one lemon, one shot glass of cognac and a tiny spoonful of powdered ginger.

Cut chicken filets in cubes for brochettes and leeks into round slices.

Slide alternating pieces of chicken and leek onto wooden skewers.

Marinate brochettes for 1 hour in Teriyaki sauce. Baste often.

- Cut the chicken filets into cubes for brochettes.
- Wash leeks; discard dark green leaf parts. Slice white, yellow and pale green portions into rounds.
- Alternate pieces of chicken and leek on wooden skewers.
- Marinate for 1 hour in Teriyaki sauce. Baste often.
- Preheat browning dish or plate for 5 to 6 minutes.
- Brown the brochettes in the microwave. Turn often to expose all sides.
- Continue cooking according to chart instructions. Rotate brochettes a quarter turn every 2 minutes.
- When brochettes attain a nice brown color, let stand and serve.

Leek is used here essentially as garnish. It may still be slightly undercooked when the chicken is done, so may appeal only to those who enjoy crunchy vegetables.

CURRIED CHICKEN

Servings	•4/5	• 6/8•
Setting	+ + +	+ + +
500 watts	min 10	min 15
600/650 watts	9	13 1/2
700 watts	8	13 1/2
Standing Time	5	7
Calories	420	
Fat Content	Quite Low (27 g)	
Utensil: Shallow Cooking Dish	2 qt (2 l)	4 qt (4 l)
Ingredients		
Chicken wings or Chicken legs (small or large)	8 5	14 8
Grated apple	1 cup	2 cups
Grated coconut	1/2 cup	1 cup
Grated onion	1/2 cup	1 cup
Dried raisins	1/4 cup	1/2 cup
Dark rum	3 tbsp	5 tbsp
Coconut milk	1/4 cup	1/2 cup
Whipping cream	1/2 cup	1 cup
Curry powder	2 tbsp	3 tbsp
Salt	1 tsp	1 1/2 tsp

Soak raisins in rum; combine all other ingredients. Grate apple and onion.

Coat each chicken piece with curry.

Mix all ingredients for the sauce.

Arrange chicken pieces on cooking dish and cover with sauce.

- Soak raisins in rum.
- Grate apples and onion.
- Coat each chicken piece with curry powder.
- Mix together grated apples and onion, grated coconut, marinated raisins and rum, coconut milk, cream, salt and the rest of the curry. Stir well.
- Arrange chicken pieces on cooking dish. Spread sauce over chicken pieces.
- Cover and cook in microwave according to chart instructions.
- Half way through cooking process, turn chicken pieces over and stir sauce. Complete cooking process.
- During standing time, run sauce through blender and through sieve, as shown on p. 29. Pour over chicken before serving.

This recipe has been adapted for microwave cooking from a great classic dish from the Indes. Serve with rice.

Chicken legs in coarse salt

Servings	2	4
Setting	+ + +	+ + +
500 watts	min 7	min 12
600/650 watts	$6^1/_2$	11
700 watts	6	$10^1/_2$
Standing Time	4	6
Calories	200	
Fat Content	Low (10 g)	
Utensil: Plastic Cooking Pouch		
Ingredients		
Small chicken legs	4	8
Coarse Salt	2 cups	4 cups
Paprika	$^1/_4$ tsp	$^1/_2$ tsp
Green bean salad	As accompanying dish	

Choose small, very lean chicken legs.

Combine coarse salt and paprika in a bowl.

Pour this mixture in a cooking pouch and add chicken pieces.

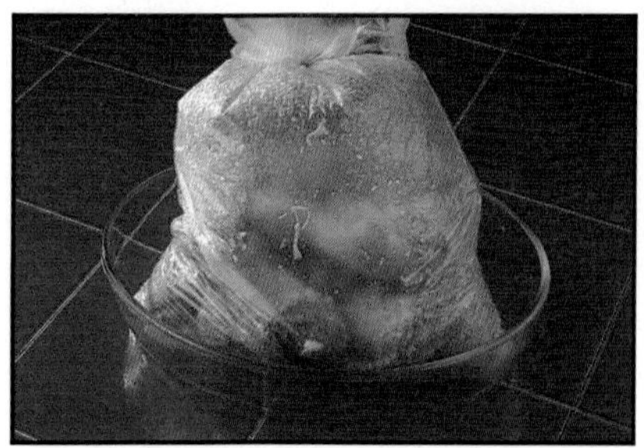

Use string to close cooking pouch and shake well to coat all pieces with salt.

- Choose small, very lean chicken legs (This recipe is prepared without fat, and you do not want to lose this advantage by using fatty chicken).
- Combine coarse salt and paprika in a bowl.
- Pour this ''pink'' salt into a cooking pouch.
- Add chicken pieces.
- Tie cooking pouch with string and shake well to coat all of chicken.
- Cook in microwave on a gratin dish or other plate according to chart instructions.
- The pouch will puff up during cooking process. Punch a hole in it half way through cooking time and turn chicken pieces over. Complete cooking process. Let stand. Shake all excess salt particles off chicken. Serve with green bean salad with a garlic and vinegar dressing.

This is by far the simplest recipe in this book, and one of the most delicious as well. Even though the chicken cooks in salt, it will not taste at all salty.

ROAST DUCK

Servings	•4/5	• 6/8•
Setting	+ + +	+ + +
500 watts	min 18	min 26
600/650 watts	17	25
700 watts	16	24
Standing Time	6	8
Calories	400	
Fat Content	Average (30 g)	
Utensil: Trivet (*see p. 19*)		
Ingredients		
Duck (Not too fat)	4 lbs (1.8 kg)	6 lbs (2.7 kg)
Soya sauce	1/2 cup	1 cup
Paprika	1 tbsp	2 tbsp
Pepper	1 tsp	2 tsp
Vegetable medly as accompanying dish		

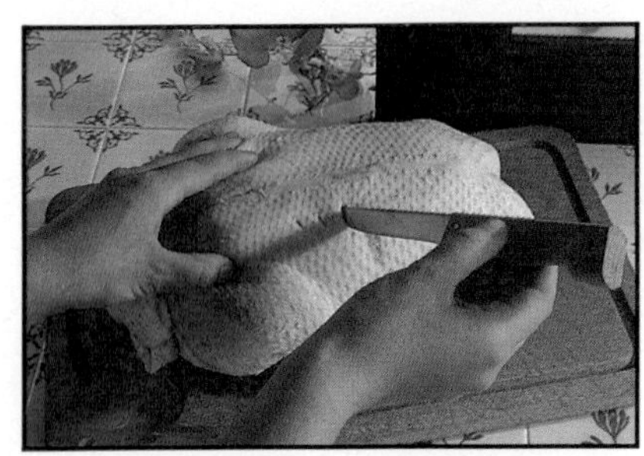

Slit duck skin to allow excess fat to escape during cooking.

Combine soya sauce, paprika and pepper.

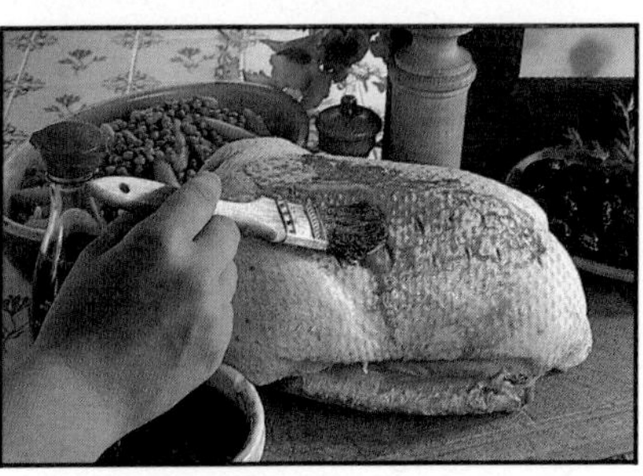

Baste duck with soya sauce mixture using a kitchen brush. It will give duck a lovely golden color and added flavor.

Set duck on a trivet (see p. 19) or on any arrangement of cookware allowing fat to drain away from meat during cookig process.

- Choose a duck that is not too fat.
- With sharp knife, make small slits in skin. Excess fat will drain out of these slits during cooking process, making the duck tastier and easier to digest.
- Mix paprika, pepper and soya sauce.
- Baste entire duck with this mixture. It will give the duck a golden coloring and added flavor.
- Set duck on a trivet dish to prevent it cooking in its own juices. A plate set upside down in a dish will produce the same effect.
- Cook in microwave according to chart directions. Half way through cooking process, turn duck over for uniform cooking and browning.
- You can also cut duck in two to accelerate cooking, but the presentation may not be as attractive.
- Let duck stand, then serve with vegetable medley garnished with black olives and tarragon. The final pleasure of the process is carving the duck at the table and making your guests' mouths water.

If you prefer your duck rare, reduce cooking time by 5 minutes.

Duck Filets with Cherries

Servings	• 1	• 2 •
Setting	+ + +	+ + +
500 watts	min 4	min 6
600/650 watts	$3^3/4$	$5^1/2$
700 watts	$3^1/2$	5
Standing Time	3	4

Calories	520
Fat Content	Average (33 g)

Utensil: Browning Dish

Ingredients		
Filet(s) of duck reasonably lean, medium size,	1	2
Liquid honey	2 tbsp	4 tbsp
Cucumbers	$^1/2$ lb (225 g)	1 lb (450 g)
Cherries in syrup	$^1/2$ cup	1 cup
Vinegar	1 tsp	2 tsp
Pepper	$^1/4$ tsp	$^1/2$ tsp
Powdered ginger	$^1/4$ tsp	$^1/2$ tsp
Salt	$^1/4$ tsp	$^1/2$ tsp

Slice through skin diagonally and in both directions to produce more evenly cooked meat.

Combine vinegar, salt, pepper, ginger and honey. Baste meat with this mixture.

Preheat browning dish for 7 minutes and brown filets first on one side, then on the other.

- With a very sharp knife, cut fine, diagonal slits in duck skin in both directions to allow more even cooking of meat.
- Dissolve salt in vinegar. Add pepper, ginger and honey. Mix well.
- Baste filets with this mixture.
- With an apple-corer, form cucumber balls the size of cherries. (Use remaining cucumber in a salad).
- Preheat browning dish 7 minutes and broil duck filets on meat side; repeat process on skin side.
- Add cucumber marbles, cherries, one or two spoonfuls of cherry syrup and the rest of the honey mixture.
- Cover and continue cooking process.
- During standing time indicated for duck, finish cooking the sauce, cucumbers and cherries. Serve immediately.

It would be presumptuous to state that the cooking times given here will always produce perfect results; each duck reacts differently to cooking. The only solution is to keep a very close watch on cooking times.

Quail with Grapes

Servings	1	2
Setting	+ + + and + +	+ + + and + +
500 watts	min 6	min 10
600/650 watts	$5^3/_4$	$9^1/_2$
700 watts	$5^1/_2$	9
Standing Time	3	4
Calories	300	
Fat Content	Negligeable	
Utensil: Oval Gratin Dish	1 qt (1 l)	$1^1/_2$ qts (1.5 l)
Ingredients		
Small quail $^1/_3$ lb (150 g) each	2	4
Fresh grapes	$^1/_2$ cup	1 cup
Grape juice	$^1/_4$ cup	$^1/_2$ cup
Vinegar	1 tbsp	2 tbsp
Sugar	1 tbsp	2 tbsp
Pepper	$^1/_4$ tsp	$^1/_2$ tsp
Salt	$^1/_4$ tsp	$^1/_2$ tsp

Choose small plump quail not exceeding $^1/_3$ lb (150 g).

Combine grape juice, vinegar, sugar, salt and pepper in cooking dish and marinate quail in juice for 1 hour.

Peel grapes and set in a bowl.

Pour quail marinade into bowl.

- The best quail is plump, but not too fatty and should weigh from $^1/_3$ lb (150 g) à $^1/_2$ lb (225 g) at the most.
- Combine grape juice, vinegar, sugar, salt and pepper in the cooking dish.
- Marinate quail in this mixture for one hour.
- Peel grapes and set them in a bowl.
- Add the quail marinade to the bowl.
- Put quail in gratin dish and grapes in bowl in microwave at same time.
- Cook according to chart instructions, starting on HIGH, then switching to MEDIUM half way through cooking process.
- Cut quail in half. Let stand then set on plates; garnish with grapes and cover with sauce mixture.

You could also make this recipe using chicken wings instead of quail.

MEATS

If you use the browning plate to brown a piece of meat that requires long cooking, be sure to transfer the meat to another cooking container to finish cooking, because browning dishes absorb a great deal of energy.
Never salt meat before cooking; it dries it out. On the other hand you can pepper it liberally.
Never cook a roast without making sure it is raised off the bottom of the dish so it doesn't stew in its own juice. There is a special microwave utensil, the trivet, designed for this purpose. (*See p. 19.*) It also permits you to collect the fat and juice easily. If you do not have a *trivet*, you can make do with a saucer turned upside down in the cooking dish to keep the meat off the bottom.
If you want to be sure to avoid any possible mistakes when cooking meat in the microwave, be sure to read carefully the basic information in the introductory chapter (*pages 10 to 41*).

COOKING CHART

FOOD	WEIGHT	COOKING TIME (MIN) 500W	600/650W	700W	POWER SETTING
BEEF					
Ground meat	1 lb (450 g)	6 min	5½ min	5 min	+ + +
Steak , "blue"	½ lb (225 g)	2½ min	2¼ min	2 min	+ + +
Steak, rare	½ lb (225 g)	3 min	2¾ min	2½ min	+ + +
Steak, medium	½ lb (225 g)	3⅔ min	3¼ min	3 min	+ + +
Steak, well done	½ lb (225 g)	4½ min	4 min	3¾ min	+ + +
Roast, "blue"	per lb (450 g)	13 min	11 min	10½ min	+ +**
Roast, rare	per lb (450 g)	16 min	13½ min	12 min	+ +**
Roast, medium	per lb (450 g)	18 min	15 min	13½ min	+ +**
Roast, well done	per lb (450 g)	20 min	17 min	15½ min	+ +**
PORK					
Bacon, sliced	½ lb (225 g)	5 min	4½ min	4 min	+ + +
Chops	1 lb (450 g)	15 min	13½ min	12 min	+ +
Roast	per lb (450 g)	17 min	15 min	13 min	+ +
Spare Ribs	per lb (450 g)	20 min	18 min	16 min	+ +
Ham	per lb (450 g)	13 min	12 min	11 min	+ +
VEAL					
Roast	per lb (450 g)	20 min	17 min	15 min	++
Chops	for 4	6 min	5 min	4 min	++
LAMB					
Chops	for 4	6 min	5 min	4 min	+ +
Leg or Shoulder***	per lb (450 g)	17 min	15 min	13 min	+ +
	well done	21 min	18 min	15½ min	+ +

It is important to turn meat often during cooking. (*see p. 30.*) Cook large pieces of meat at half power (MEDIUM power setting) especially if you like interior pink.
Don't forget that the fattier the cut of meat, the faster it cooks. Take this into account when adjusting the cooking time given on the cooking chart.

Remember that it is always better to undercook meat a little than to overcook it, as the cooking process is not reversible.
The cooking times given on the chart apply to the first lb (450 g) of weight. Subtract 2 minutes from this for the second lb, and 4 minutes for each additional lb (450 g).
For example, to cook a 4 lb (1.8 kg) roast "blue" (very rare) in a 600/650W microwave, calculate as follows:

1st lb	–	11 min
2nd lb	–	9 min
3rd lb	–	7 min
4th lb	–	7 min
Total		34 min

**
See photos p. 160.

***
Subtract the same number of minutes for other meats as for beef when calculating for additional lbs.

Cooking Meat

Cooking meat, especially beef, in an important skill to master. People who like their steak on the rare side react to well done steak as they would to a piece of cardboard. On the other hand, those who like their steak medium won't be very happy if you serve it to them 'blue'.

Therefore, it's important to be precise both for the selection of cooking time (as we have tried to do on p. 161) and for the choice of technique.

Since everything to do with gastronomy is to some degree subjective, let us make sure that we understand the meaning of the terms used in this section.

The five photos on this page, taken of the same roast at different stages of cooking, will help us be sure that we are talking the same language.

' Blue '

' Rare '

' Medium-Rare '

' Medium '

' Well Done '

Preparation of Meatballs

Ground meat adapts very well to microwave cooking; it is a practical food that cooks fast and can be adapted to a number of recipes.

Several of the recipes in the following section are based on ground meat, whether shaped into meatballs are not.

For such recipes, there is a particularly delicious ground meat mixture which is equally good on its own.

The basic ground meat mixture is a follows:

1 lb (450 g) beef
1 lb (450 g) turkey filet
1 lb (450 g) sausage meat
1 cup bread crumbs soaked in milk
1 cup chopped onion
1 tbsp chopped garlic
1/2 cup chopped parsley
1/2 chopped green pepper
3 eggs
2 tbsp hot French mustard
1 tsp paprika
1 tsp pepper (or to taste)
1 tsp salt (or to taste)

Put all ingredients in the food processor and process just until coarse.

Shape meatballs into desired size. Roll in flour.

Cook in the microwave between two sheets of wax paper. Plan on about 5 minutes at HIGH for 8 meatballs of 2 oz (60 g) each. You can also fry them in a little oil brought to the boiling point.

RIB ROAST IN WHITE WINE

Servings	•5/6	•8/10•
Setting	+ +	+ +
500 watts	min 42	min 70
600/650 watts	34	53
700 watts	30	46
Standing Time*	10	15
Calories	600	
Fat Content	High (55 g)	
Utensil: Bowl and *trivet* (*see p. 19*)		
Ingredients		
Beef Rib Roast	3 lbs (1,4 kg)	5 lbs (2,3 kg)
Browning Mixture (*See pp. 32, 33*)	1/2 cup	1 cup
Dry white wine	1/2 cup	1 cup
Sliced mushrooms	1 cup	1 1/2 cups
Chopped onion	1/2 cup	3/4 cup
Thin slices of bacon	6	10
Whipping cream	2/3 cup	1 cup
Chopped tarragon	1 tbsp	1 1/2 tbsp
Powdered sugar	1 tbsp	1 1/2 tbsp
Coarse-ground pepper	1 tbsp	1 1/2 tbsp
Salt	1 tsp	1 1/2 tsp

* Standing Time for meat and cooking time for sauce.

Baste roast on all sides with browning mixture. Cook on trivet set on microwave turntable.

Ingredients for sauce: thinly sliced mushrooms and bacon, chopped tarragon and onion.

Cook sauce in microwave while roast is standing.

- Baste roast on all sides with browning mixture. Place roast on *trivet*; set *trivet* on microwave turntable (*see p. 31*).
- Cover with wax paper and cook in microwave at medium according to chart directions.
- Slice mushrooms and bacon thin.
- Chop onion and tarragon.
- When meat is cooked, pull out of microwave, cover and let stand.
- Put onion, bacon and mushrooms in bowl or small casserole. Cook in microwave on HIGH for 3 minutes. Add sugar, salt and pepper. Pour white wine into mixture. Cover and cook 5 minutes longer.
- Add cream and tarragon. Reduce oven setting to MEDIUM and simmer while you carve meat after its designated standing time.
- Pour sauce over meat and serve immediately.

A marvellous sauce to enhance a delectable cut of meat!

BEEF CHOP SUEY

Servings	2	4
Setting	+ + +	+ + +
500 watts	min 6	min 10
600/650 watts	5 1/2	9 1/2
700 watts	5	9
Standing Time	3	4
Calories	320	
Fat Content	Low (14 g)	
Utensil: Round Cooking Dish	1 qt (1 l)	2 qts (2 l)
Ingredients		
Beef Filet	1/2 lb (225 g)	1 lb (450 g)
Medium size red pepper	1/2	1
Medium size green pepper	1/2	1
Drained bamboo shoots	1/4 cup	1/2 cup
Bean sprouts	1/2 cup	1 cup
Green beans	1/4 cup	1/2 cup
Chopped parsley	1 tbsp	2 tbsp
Chopped chives	1 tsp	2 tsp
Chopped garlic	1 tsp	2 tsp
Lemon juice	1 tsp	2 tsp
Soya sauce	2 tbsp	4 tbsp
Powdered sugar	1 tsp	2 tsp
Powdered ginger	1/2 tsp	1 tsp
Cayenne pepper	1/8 tsp	1/4 tsp
Salt	1/4 tsp	1/2 tsp

Choose a good filet of beef and very fresh vegetables.

Cut thin slices of beef.

Chop vegetables into small cubes. Chop garlic, parsley and chives.

Two-thirds of the way into cooking time, add beef slices, cover with sauce and stir.

- Choose a good beef filet and very fresh vegetables.
- Cut thin slices of beef, the size of french fries.
- Cut peppers and bamboo shoots into small cubes. Slice green beans into fine sticks. Chop garlic, parsley and chives.
- Put all vegetables in cooking dish along with garlic, parsley and chives. Pour lemon juice and soya sauce over vegetables. Add sugar, ginger, cayenne pepper and salt. Stir.
- Cover and cook in microwave according to chart instructions.
- Two-thirds of the way into cooking time, uncover and add beef slices. Cover with sauce, stir and complete cooking process.
- Serve at the end of standing time with accompanying dish of white rice.

A delicious chinese dish, fool-proof in microwave!

Beef with Carrots

Servings	4	6
Setting	+ + + and + +	+ + + and + +
500 watts	min 80	min 90
600/650 watts	78	87
700 watts	76	84
Standing Time	7	10
Calories	390	
Fat Content	Quite Low (26 g)	
Utensil: Shallow Round Dish	2 qts (2 l)	3 qts (3 l)
Ingredients		
Beef Rib Roast	$1^1/_2$ lbs (675 g)	$2^1/_4$ lbs (1 kg)
Good red wine	1 cup	$1^1/_2$ cup
Carrots cut into rounds	$1^1/_2$ cups	2 cups
Sliced onion	$^1/_2$ cup	$^3/_4$ cup
Beef consommé	1 cup	$1^1/_2$ cup
Chopped garlic	1 tsp	$1^1/_2$ tsp
Chopped thyme	1 tsp	$1^1/_2$ tsp
Bay leaf(ves)	1 leaf	2 leaves
Pepper	1 tsp	$1^1/_2$ tsp
Salt	1 tsp	$1^1/_2$ tsp

Cut meat into 1 inch (28 mm) cubes.

Arrange meat in dish with vegetables and seasonings. Pour red wine over mixture and marinate for 2 hours.

Take meat out of marinade; its cooking time is shorter than that of carrots and sauce.

- Cut meat into 1 inch (28 mm) square cubes.
- Set meat on plate.
- Add sliced carrots, sliced onion, chopped thyme, crushed bay leaves, garlic, salt and pepper.
- Pour red wine into mixture.
- Marinate for 2 hours, covered; stir every 15 minutes with a wooden spoon.
- At the end of this time, take out cubed meat and add beef consommé. Stir and cover with plastic wrap with one or two small perforations.
- Cook in microwave for 1 hour on HIGH, stirring occasionally.
- Add meat pushing it under sliced carrots and sauce. Set oven at MEDIUM and complete cooking process according to chart instructions.
- Let stand before serving.

Once again, the microwave oven proves to be a wonderful tool for simmering foods. Even our grandmothers would have approved!

Virginia Beef Steak

Servings	• 4/6 •	
Setting	+ + + Rare	Well Done
500 watts	min 14	min 17
600/650 watts	13	16
700 watts	12	15
Standing Time	7	7
Calories	470	
Fat Content	Average (38 g)	
Utensil: Oval Gratin Dish	1 1/2 qts (1.5 l)	

Ingredients	
Tender cut of boneless steak	2 lbs (900 g)
Turkey Filet	1/2 lb (225 g)
Red pepper	1
Green pepper	1
Smoked sausage, medium size	1
Pepper	1/2 tsp
Salt	1/2 tsp
Browning Mixture	1/2 cup
Mustard with horseradish or Japanese Wassabi	2 tbsp (or 1 tbsp Wassabi)
Whipping cream	1/2 cup
Chopped tarragon	1 tbsp

Slice steak through middle, without cutting all the way through.

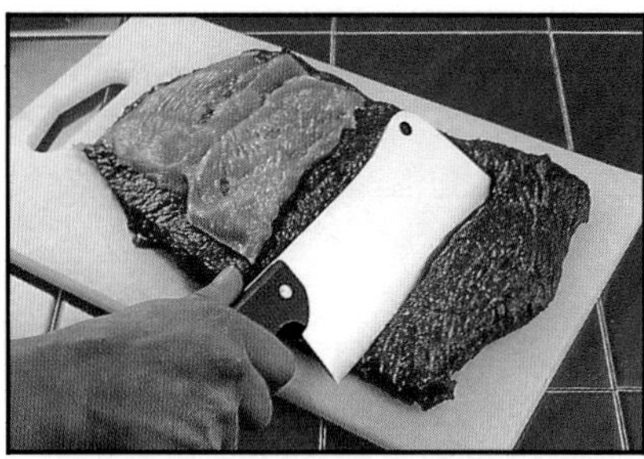

Pound vigorously to flatten.

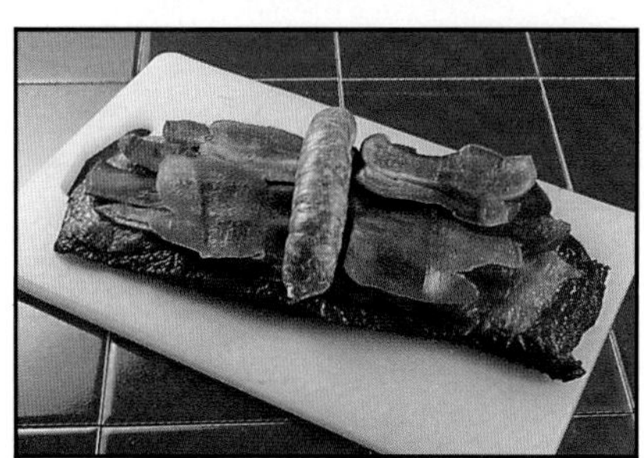

Add thin slices of turkey, pepper strips and sausage. Season between each layer.

Roll and tie as indicated on page 137. During standing time for meat, prepare horseradish mustard sauce.

- Slice steak through middle, without cutting all the way through. Spread open.
- Pound vigorously to flatten.
- Sprinkle with salt and pepper.
- Cover with a layer of thinly sliced turkey filet. Sprinkle lightly with salt and pepper.
- Clean out pepper seeds and remove white membranes; cut into thin strips and arrange over turkey filet.
- Arrange smoked sausage in middle.
- Roll and tie securely as shown on p. 137.
- Baste roll with browning mixture and cook in microwave according to chart instructions, wrapped in plastic wrap.
- During standing time for meat, prepare sauce: whip horseradish mustard (or Japanese wassabi) with cream. Sprinkle with tarragon before serving.

Hot or cold, this Virginia Beef Steak is delicious. An added attraction to any picnic.

S
P

Pork Spareribs

Servings	2	4
Setting	++	++
500 watts	min 20	min 40
600/650 watts	18	36
700 watts	16	32
Standing Time	5	7
Calories	360	
Fat Content	Quite Low (29 g)	
Utensil: Rectangular Gratin dish	$1^1/2$ qts (1.5 l)	$2^1/2$ qts (2,5 l)
Ingredients		
Pork spareribs	1 lb (450 g)	2 lbs (900 g)
Lemon juice	1 tbsp	2 tbsp
Soya sauce	2 tbsp	4 tbsp
Chopped garlic	1 tsp	2 tsp
Brown sugar	2 tbsp	4 tbsp
Oil	1 tbsp	2 tbsp
Paprika	1 tsp	2 tsp
Tabasco sauce	2 drops	4 drops
Salt	$^1/2$ tsp	1 tsp

Choose lean spareribs. Prepare ingredients for basting.

Thoroughly combine lemon juice, soya sauce, chopped garlic, brown sugar, oil, paprika, tabasco sauce and salt in a bowl.

Baste spareribs on all sides with this mixture. Their flavor will improve and they will turn golden and crispy.

- Choose lean spareribs; if too fatty, remove excess fat with sharp knife. If very bony, you can increase quantities without changing cooking time.
- Combine thoroughly lemon juice, soya sauce, chopped garlic, brown sugar, oil, paprika, tabasco sauce and salt in a bowl.
- Baste spareribs on all sides with mixture.
- Arrange meat in a plate, preferably along the outer edges (they will cook better and more evenly).
- Cook in microwave according to chart instructions.
- Turn dish every 10 minutes and baste spareribs with sauce. At the end of cooking time, they will be a lovely golden color; serve immediately after standing time or use them in another recipe.

Despite its high fat content, this savory cut of meat is not really fattening as there are more bones than meat. Make sure the ribs are well browned.

Pork Spareribs with Orange

Servings	2	4
Setting	+ + +	+ + +
500 watts	min 16	min 20
600/650 watts	15	19
700 watts	14	18
Standing Time	6	8
Calories	480	
Fat Content	Average (32 g)	
Utensil: Pyrex Bowl or Casserole	$1\frac{1}{2}$ qts (1.5 l)	2 qts (2 l)
Ingredients		
Roasted pork spareribs	1 lb (450 g)	2 lbs (900 g)
Orange marmalade	2 tbsp	4 tbsp
Red currant jelly	2 tbsp	4 tbsp
Soya sauce	1 tbsp	2 tbsp
Wine vinegar	2 tbsp	4 tbsp
Orange	1/2	1
Tomato(es)	1	2
Green pepper	1/2	1
Chopped onion	1 tbsp	2 tbsp
Powdered ginger	1/2 tsp	1 tsp
Tabasco sauce	3 drops	6 drops
Salt	1/4 tsp	1/2 tsp

Prepare and cook spareribs exactly as indicated in preceding recipe.

Cut spareribs apart between bones. Prepare sauce and chop vegetables.

The finished product, ready to enjoy.

- Prepare and cook spareribs exactly as directed in preceding recipe.
- Cut spareribs apart between each bone.
- Combine orange marmalade, red currant jelly, soya sauce, vinegar, ginger, tabasco sauce and salt.
- Chop pepper and tomato(es) into small pieces.
- Peel and cut up orange.
- Chop onion.
- Put meat in cooking container. Pour sauce over meat; add peppers, tomato(es), orange and onion.
- Stir. Cover and cook in microwave according to chart directions.
- Serve at the end of standing time.

A most appetizing recipe for spareribs, with delicate oriental undertones.

ROAST PORK WITH APPLES

Servings	4	6
Setting	+ +	+ +
	min	min
500 watts	25	38
600/650 watts	22	33
700 watts	19	29
Standing Time	8	10

Calories	540
Fat Content	Average (34 g)

Utensil: Browning Dish

Ingredients		
Pork roast	$1^1/2$ lb (675 g)	$2^1/4$ lbs (1 kg)
Applesauce	16 oz (450 ml)	24 oz (675 ml)
Powdered cinnamon	1 tsp	$1^1/2$ tsp
Raisins	1/4 cup	1/2 cup
Calvados (or brandy)	2 tbsp	3 tbsp
Pepper	1/2 tsp	3/4 tsp
Salt	1/2 tsp	3/4 tsp
Butter	1 tbsp	1/2 tbsp
Browning Mixture (*see p. 30*)	1/2 cup	1/2 cup

Soak raisins in Calvados or brandy.

Combine cinnamon and applesauce.

Brown roast on the browning plate. Add butter and pepper.

- Soak raisins in Calvados or brandy.
- Combine cinnamon and applesauce.
- Preheat browning plate in microwave oven for 7 minutes.
- Baste roast pork with browning mixture.
- Brown on all sides in browning dish. Add butter and sprinkle with pepper.
- Continue to cook in microwave according to chart instructions.
- Arrange applesauce and Calvados-soaked raisins around roast 8 minutes before the end of cooking process. Salt, cover and complete cooking process. Stir once or twice.
- Serve after standing time.

Pork, apples, Calvados and cinnamon are ideal complements to each other and in this recipe, they harmonize perfectly.

HAM WITH PORT

Servings	1	2
Setting	+ + +	+ + +
	min	min
500 watts	4	6
600/650 watts	$3^1/2$	$5^1/2$
700 watts	$3^1/4$	5
Standing Time	2	4

Calories	590
Fat Content	Quite High (40 g)

Utensils: Plate and bowl or small casserole

Ingredients		
Cooked ham slice(s), quite thick	1	2
Cornstarch	1/2 tsp	1 tsp
Port	2 tbsp	4 tbsp
Light cream (10% m.g.)	1/4 cup	1/2 cup
Paprika	1/4 tsp	1/2 tsp
Pepper	1/8 tsp	1/4 tsp
Salt	1/8 tsp	1/4 tsp
Browning mixture (see p. 30)	3 tbsp	5 tbsp

Season cream with paprika, salt and pepper. Mix cornstarch in spoonful of water.

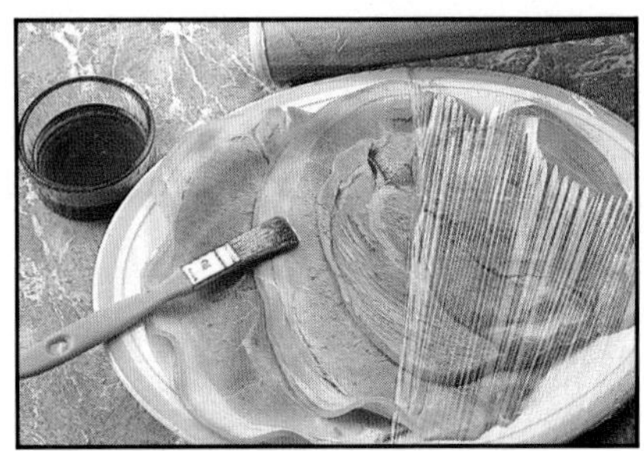

Baste ham slices with browning mixture and cover plate with plastic wrap.

Cook sauce on top shelf and ham on bottom of microwave oven simultaneously.

- Season cream with paprika, salt and pepper.
- Mix cornstarch in spoonful of water.
- Baste ham slice(s) with browning mixture (a combination of maple syrup, and soya sauce, for example).
- Arrange ham slice(s) on plate.
- Cover plate with plastic wrap.
- Pour port into bowl. Set in microwave on shelf for one-third cooking time indicated on chart. Remove port and flambé.
- Add cornstarch paste to bowl of port. Cover and cook in microwave. On bottom of microwave oven, set ham. Cook ham and port mixture for the second third of cooking time indicated on chart.
- Add cream to the port mixture and stir. Cover. Turn ham plate one-quarter turn and cook both for the final third of cooking time.
- Serve ham slice(s) covered with port sauce.

Do not hesitate to use a very fine brand of port. In culinary art, inexpensive substitutes are costlier in taste and enjoyment. For want of a good port, use Madeira.

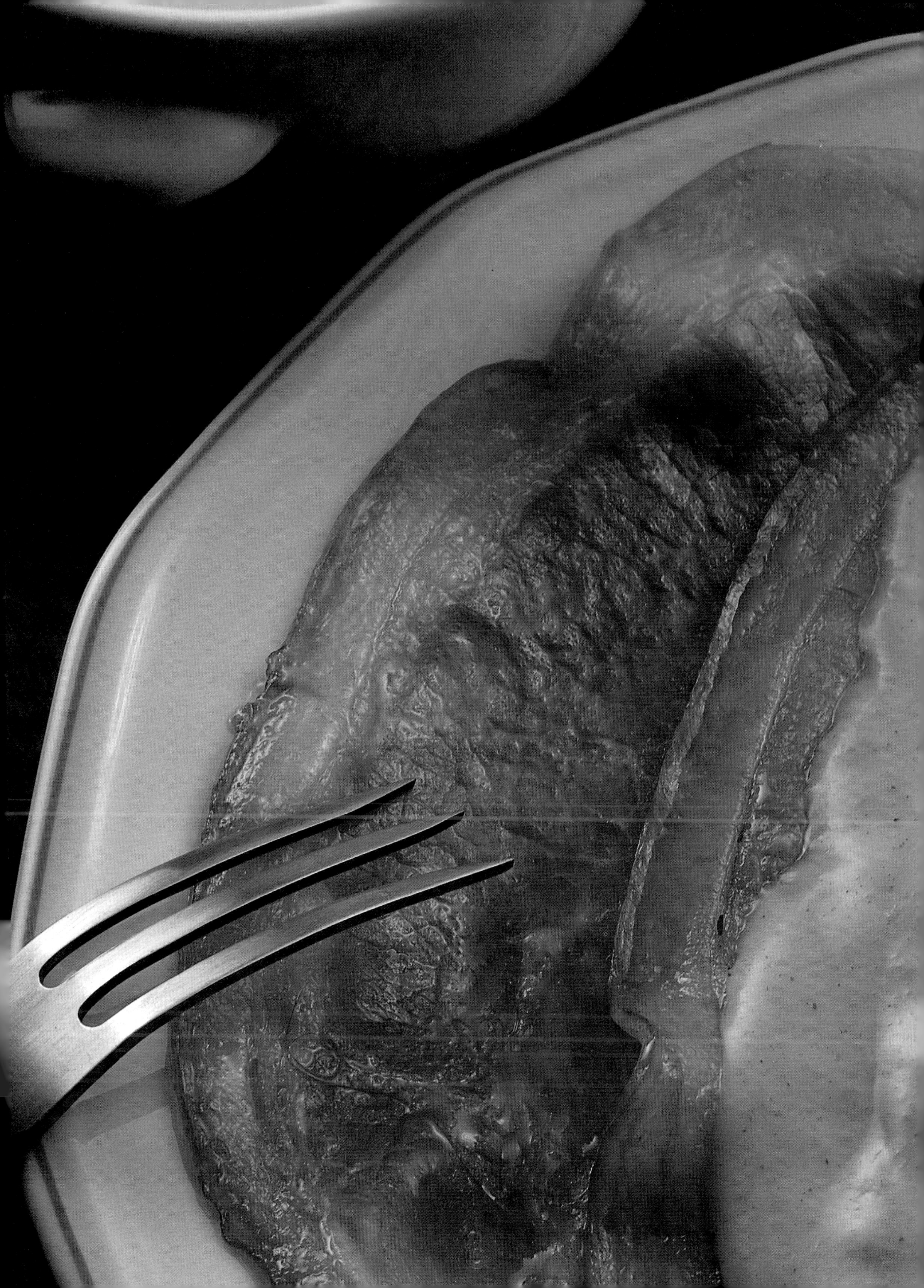

APRICOT-GLAZED HAM

Servings	•5/6	• 8/9•
Setting	+ +	+ +
500 watts	min 22	min 33
600/650 watts	21	$31^1/2$
700 watts	20	30
Standing Time	8	10

Calories	480
Fat Content	Average (32 g)

Utensils: Casserole and Cooking Pouch

Ingredients		
Cooked ham	2 lbs (900 g)	3 lbs (1,4 kg)
Apricot juice	1 cup	$1^1/2$ cups
Honey	$^1/4$ cup	$^1/2$ cup
Soya sauce	4 tbsp	6 tbsp
Lemon juice	1 tbsp	$1^1/2$ tbsp
Tabasco sauce	5 drops	8 drops
Salt	To taste	
Fresh or canned apricots, sliced in half and pitted (optional)	5	8

Choose an evenly shaped piece of cooked ham.

In a bowl, blend apricot juice, honey, soya sauce, lemon juice, tabasco sauce and salt.

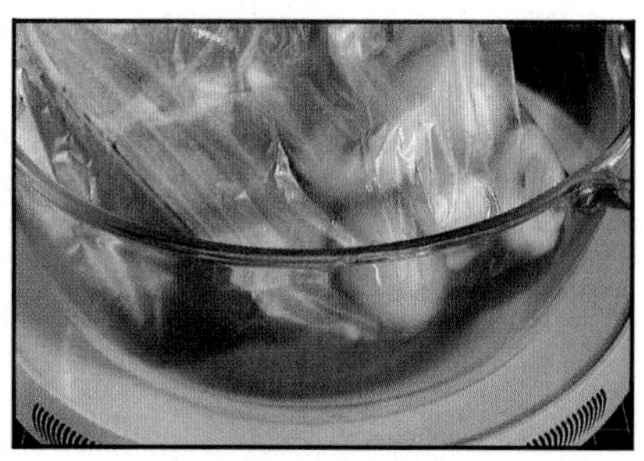

Put ham into cooking pouch with sauce. Place pouch in a casserole on microwave turntable.

- Choose an evenly shaped piece of cooked ham.
- In a bowl, blend apricot juice, honey, soya sauce, lemon juice, tabasco sauce and salt. Whip until honey is completely dissolved.
- Put ham into cooking pouch. Pour sauce into pouch and add apricot halves. Close pouch; perforate top to allow steam to escape.
- Place pouch in casserole and place in microwave, preferably on a turntable, and cook according to chart instructions.
- Shake the pouch every 5 minutes in order to baste ham completely.
- Place glazed ham on table, carve and serve.

Such a simple dish to prepare and so appetizing to look at. A delight to the palate.

Crown Roast of Lamb with Mint

Servings	• 5/6 •
Setting	+ + +
	min
500 watts	26
600/650 watts	24
700 watts	22
Standing Time	7
Calories	420
Fat Content	Quite High (42 g)
Utensils: bowl and trivet (*see p. 19*)	
Ingredients	
Loin of Lamb with 10 or 12 ribs	1
Browing mixture (lightly salted)	1/2 cup
Wine vinegar	8 tbsp
Water	4 tbsp
Powdered sugar	3 tbsp
Salt	1/4 tsp
Chopped fresh mint	3 tbsp
Chopped fresh tarragon	1 tbsp
Pepper	1/4 tsp

Ask butcher to shape loin of lamb into a crown to ensure even cooking. Protect tips ot bones with aluminum foil.

Baste crown roast of lamb with browning mixture.

To prepare mint sauce, blend vinegar, water, sugar and salt; chop fresh mint and tarragon.

- Ask butcher to shape the loin of lamb into a crown to ensure even cooking.
- Protect tips of bones with aluminum foil.
- Baste the roast with browning mixture.
- In bowl, pour vinegar, water, salt and sugar.
- Place crown roast of lamb on trivet in microwave, preferably on turntable, and cook according to chart instructions.
- At the same time, cook vinegar mixture in microwave.
- Observe mixture carefully and remove from oven as soon as it is reduced by half. Set aside.
- Allow cooked roast to stand. Meanwhile bring vinegar mixture to a boil, remove from microwave immediately and add pepper, chopped mint and tarragon. Stir. Serve as accompaniment to the roast.

This British-inspired sauce, truly an aristocratic condiment, serves here to garnish a modern-day culinary delight.

Lamb Chops with Green Peppercorns

Servings	1	2
Setting	+ +	+ +
500 watts	min 6	min 9
600/650 watts	5 1/2	8 1/2
700 watts	5	8
Standing Time	3	4
Calories	540	
Fat Content	High (50 g)	
Utensil: Round Casserole	1/2 qt (0.5 l)	1 qt (1 l)
Ingredients		
Lamb chops	2	4
Whipping cream	2 tbsp	4 tbsp
Hot French mustard	1 tsp	2 tsp
Cognac	1 tsp	2 tsp
Drained green peppercorns	1 tsp	2 tsp
Salt	1/8 tsp	1/4 tsp
Red currants or cranberries (optional)	To garnish	

Choose lean lamb chops. If required, trim off excess fat.

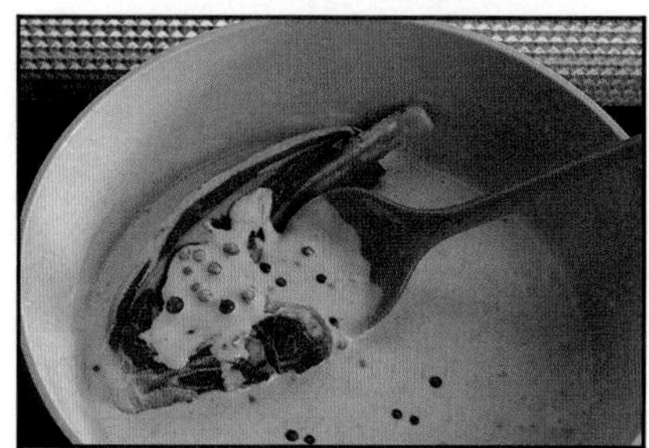

Mix cream, mustard, cognac, green peppercorns and salt. Add to lamb chops.

Coat lamb chops completely with sauce and cover dish before cooking.

- Choose lean lamb chops. A little fat is not an indication of poor quality but it may affect the taste and nutritional value. Should they be somewhat fatty, simply cut away excess fat with sharp knife.
- In the casserole, mix cream, mustard, cognac, green peppercorns and salt. Whip lightly.
- Add lamb chops and coat them well.
- Cover dish with lid and cook in microwave according to chart instructions.
- Half-way through cooking process, turn lamb chops over and stir sauce. Complete cooking process.
- While meat is standing, whip sauce vigorously for a few seconds to obtain a creamy frothy texture.
- Serve lamb chops coated with green peppercorn sauce. For garnish, add red currants or cranberries.

For those who prefer their meat slightly pink, simply eliminate standing time or reduce cooking time.

MEATBALL CHILI

Servings	1	2
Setting	+ + +	+ + +
500 watts	min $3^1/_2$	min $5^1/_2$
600/650 watts	$3^1/_4$	5
700 watts	3	$4^1/_2$
Standing Time	2	4
Calories	390	
Fat Content	Quite low (24 g)	
Utensil: Oval Gratin Dish	$^1/_2$ qt (0.5 l)	1 qt (1 l)
Ingredients		
Meat balls, 2 oz each (60 g)	3	6
Tomato juice	$^1/_4$ cup	$^1/_2$ cup
Lemon juice	1 tsp	2 tsp
Chopped onion	1 tbsp	2 tbsp
Chopped green pepper	2 tbsp	4 tbsp
Chopped parsley	1 tbsp	2 tbsp
Chopped thyme	1 tsp	2 tsp
Dried oregano	$^1/_2$ tsp	1 tsp
Chili powder or Cayenne pepper	$^1/_8$ tsp	$^1/_4$ tsp
Salt	$^1/_4$ tsp	$^1/_2$ tsp
Cooked red kidney beans, Canned or home-cooked	$^1/_4$ cup	$^1/_2$ cup

Prepare meatballs according to the recipe on p. 163.

In a bowl, mix tomato juice, lemon juice, chopped onion, green pepper, parsley and thyme with oregano, powdered chili and salt.

Arrange meatballs and red kidney beans in cooking dish and cover with sauce.

- Make meatballs according to recipe on p. 163.
- For the sauce, mix tomato juice, lemon juice, chopped onion and, finely chopped green pepper, chopped parsley and chopped thyme, chili powder or cayenne pepper, dried oregano and salt.
- Arrange meatballs in dish.
- Sprinkle with red kidney beans and cover with sauce. Make sure all meatballs are well covered so they do not dry up during cooking process.
- Cover with plastic wrap and cook in microwave according to chart instructions.
- Serve at the end of prescribed standing time.

A most nourishing and accelerated version of the celebrated Mexican "Chili Con Carne".

HAMBURGERS

Servings	1	2
Setting	+ + +	+ + +
500 watts	min $1^2/_3$	min $2^3/_4$
600/650 watts	$1^1/_3$	$2^1/_2$
700 watts	$1^1/_6$	$2^1/_4$
Standing Time	2	3

Calories	380	
Fat Content	Low (13 g)	
Utensil: *Trivet* (*see p. 19*)		
Ingredients		
Ground beef or Mixed ground meat	$3^1/_2$ oz (100 g)	7 oz (200 g)
Small hamburger buns	1	2
Cheese slice(s)	1	2
Tomato, average size	$^1/_2$	1
Onion, average size	$^1/_4$	$^1/_2$
Lettuce leaves	2	4
Thin slices of cucumber or Sweet-and-sour pickles	2	4
Mayonnaise, Tartar sauce, Cocktail sauce, picallili or relish	1 tbsp	2 tbsp
Hot mustard	1 tsp	2 tsp
Butter	1 tsp	2 tsp

Season ground beef or prepare ground meat according to recipe on p. 163.

Shape patties. Use a glass to cut cheese into rounds to fit patties.

Cook meat and prepare hamburgers with lettuce leaf, meat, sauce and vegetables on one half of hamburger bun. Cover with second half and serve.

- Hamburgers can be prepared in a thousand-and-one ways, according to individual tastes. Microwave cooking speeds up the process and makes the hamburgers tastier.
- Sprinkle beef with salt and pepper or simply prepare ground meat according to recipe on p. 163.
- Slice tomato, onion and cucumber or pickles into thin slices or small cubes.
- Mix butter with hot mustard.
- Shape meat into patties weighing approximately $1^3/_4$ oz (50 g) each.
- Set a cheese slice (cheddar, for example) between two patties. If slices are square, trim off edges. Use leftover cheese in another recipe.
- Arrange meat patties on *trivet*.
- Cover with wax paper. Cook in microwave according to chart indications, along with small hamburger buns.
- Let meat stand. Butter each hamburger bun on both sides with butter-mustard mixture.
- Arrange a lettuce leaf on each bun half then add meat patty, sauce of your choice and chopped mixture of tomatoes, onion and cucumber.
- Cover with second bun half and serve immediately.

All hamburger ingredients may be prepared in advance and cooked at the last minute, all within a few seconds, in microwave.

MEAT LOAF

Servings	•4/5	• 6/8•
Setting	+ + +	+ + +
500 watts	min 12	min 18
600/650 watts	11	$16^1/_2$
700 watts	10	15
Standing Time	7	10
Calories	350	
Fat Content	Low (18 g)	
Utensil: Rectagular Dish	2 qt (2 l)	3 qt (3 l)
Ingredients		
Ground beef	$1^1/_2$ lbs (675 g)	$2^1/_4$ lbs (1 kg)
Chopped mushroom	1 cup	$1^1/_2$ cups
Chopped onion	$^1/_2$ cup	$^2/_3$ cup
Chopped parsley	2 tbsp	3 tbsp
Chopped thyme	1 tsp	$1^1/_2$ tsp
Tomato sauce	$^1/_2$ cup	$^2/_3$ cup
Hot mustard	1 tbsp	$1^1/_2$ tbsp
Powdered brown sugar	2 tbsp	3 tbsp
Worcestershire sauce	2 tsp	3 tsp
Tabasco sauce	6 drops	9 drops
Salt	1 tsp	$1^1/_2$ tsp
Eggs	2	3
Glaze *(see p. 34)*	2 tbsp	3 tbsp

Assemble all ingredients.

Combine ground meat with eggs, mustard, sugar, Worcestershire sauce, Tabasco sauce and salt.

In blender, grind mushroom, onion, parsley and thyme. Add tomato sauce. Mix.

Grind all ingredients in blender and pour into cookware. Smooth with spatula.

- Chop mushroom, onion parsley and thyme.
- Grind in blender until mixture is finely ground.
- Add tomato sauce. Blend.
- Combine ground meat with eggs, mustard, sugar, Worcestershire and tabasco sauces and salt.
- Mix together ground vegetables and seasoned meat mixture. Use spatula to obtain smooth texture.
- Coat bottom of cookware with plastic wrap as indicated on p. 22.
- Pour in mixture. Flatten and smooth out with spatula.
- Pour glazing mixture over loaf and cook in microwave according to chart directions.
- When meat loaf is cooked, let stand and unmold.
- Serve hot or cold, decorated with a garnish of tomato and cucumber slices.

With light mixed green salad, this makes a delicious wholesome meal.

ROAST BEEF CANAPES

Servings	1	2
Setting	+ + +	+ + +
500 watts	min $2^1/_2$	min 4
600/650 watts	$2^1/_4$	$3^1/_2$
700 watts	2	3
Standing Time	2	3

Calories	470
Fat Content	Quite Low (23 g)

Utensil: Wax Paper

Ingredients		
Toasted bread, crusts trimmed *(see p. 37)*	2	4
Cooked roast beef slice(s) *(see p. 161)*	1	2
Thick slices of cucumber	3	6
Small spring onions with tops	2	4
Chopped fresh tarragon	1 tbsp	2 tbsp
Mayonnaise	1 tbsp	2 tbsp
Pepper	$^1/_4$ tsp	$^1/_2$ tsp
Salt	$^1/_4$ tsp	$^1/_2$ tsp

Prepare all ingredients. Cut cucumber into thick slices.

Cut cucumber and beef into matchsticks. Chop onions and tarragon.

Combine cucumber, roast beef, onion, tarragon, mayonnaise, salt and pepper.

Spread mixture over bread and cook in microwave between two sheets of wax paper.

- Cook roast beef less than you would normally, to compensate for the added cooking time in this recipe.
- Cut cucumber into thick slices, then into matchsticks.
- Cut roast beef into matchsticks.
- Coarsely chop onion and tarragon.
- Combine cucumber, beef, onion and tarragon with mayonnaise, pepper and salt.
- Spread mixture over half the toasted bread. Cover with remaining slices. Cook in microwave between two sheets of wax paper according to chart directions.
- Let stand and enjoy.

Another practical recipe you can prepare in advance and heat up at a moment's notice.

Hot dog medley

Servings	1	2
Setting	+ + +	+ + +
500 watts	min $1^1/_2$*	min $2^2/_3$*
600/650 watts	$1^1/_3$*	$2^1/_6$*
700 watts	$1^1/_6$*	$1^5/_6$*
Standing Time	2	3
Calories	300	
Fat Content	Low (15 g)	
Utensil: Cardboard plate and paper		
Ingredients		
Frankfurt Sausage	1	2
Small long bun(s)	1	2
Mustard**	1 tsb	2 tsb

* Calculate 2 minutes for reheating.

** Offer an assortment of mustards for your guests to enjoy: hot French mustard, old fashioned mustard, mustard with spices, mustard with green pepper, lime mustard, etc.

Choose fresh Frankfurt sausages, good fresh buns, and an assortment of mustards.

Split the sausages lengthwise. Cook in microwave on a paper plate covered with wax paper.

Let stand. Slip sausage into buns are reheat.

- Although this recipe is very elementary, it can be a real treat prepared with fresh imported or local sausages, good rolls and an assortment of mustards.
- Split the sausage lengthwise to prevent bursting during cooking process.
- Arrange sausage on a paper plate and cover with wax paper.
- Cook in microwave according to chart indications.
- Let stand. Place sausage in buns.
- Reheat for 2 minutes on paper towels. For more than four hot dogs, calculate 3 minutes to reheat.
- Serve immediately with a variety of mustards.

Along with the choice of mustards, you may want to present an assortment of sausages, for a very original and inexpensive meal.

To preserve the color and fresh flavor of vegetables cooked in the microwave, follow these basic rules:

- Never salt vegetables before cooking; it makes them tough. Add salt at the end of cooking.
- Cook vegetables in their own juice. Add one or two spoons of hot water to varieties that contain little water.
- Vegetables should be cooked covered to preserve their moisture content and texture.

VEGETABLES

COOKING CHART

FOOD	WEIGHT	COOKING TIME (MIN) 500W	600/650W	700W	SETTING
Artichokes	4 medium	9 min	8½ min	8 min	+ + +
Asparagus	1 lb (450 g)	8 min	7½ min	7 min	+ + +
Beets (cubed)	1 lb (450 g)	20 min	19 min	18 min	+ + +
Broccoli (flowerets)	1 lb (450 g)	10 min	9½ min	9 min	+ + +
Brussel Sprouts	1 lb (450 g)	8 min	7½ min	7 min	+ + +
Cabbage (leaves) (shredded)	1 lb (450 g) 1 lb (450 g)	11 min 7 min	10½ min 6½ min	10 min 6 min	+ + + + + +
Carrots (in rings)	1 lb (450 g)	12 min	11 min	10 min	+ + +
Cauliflower (in flowerets)	1 lb (450 g)	10 min	9½ min	9 min	+ + +
Celery Root (sliced)	1 lb (450 g)	12 min	11 min	10 min	+ + +
Corn (fresh)	(each ear)	4 min	3¾ min	3½ min	+ + +
Eggplant (sliced or diced)	1 lb (450 g)	6 min	5½ min	5 min	+ + +
Endives (split in two)	1 lb (450 g)	8 min	7½ min	7 min	+ + +
Green Beans	1 b (450 g)	10 min	9½ min	9 min	+ + +
Leeks	1 lb (450 g)	9 min	8½ min	8 min	+ + +
Legumes, dried	1 lb (450 g)	1 h + 30 min	1 h + 25 min	1 h + 20 min	+ + + + +
Lima Beans	1 lb (450 g)	7 min	6½ min	6 min	+ + +
Mushrooms (sliced)	1 lb (450 g)	6 min	5½ min	5 min	+ + +
Onions (chopped)	½ lb (225 g)	8 min	7½ min	7 min	+ + +
Pasta, fine (spaghetti, noodles, etc.)	½ lb (225 g) 1 lb (450 g)	8 min 18 min	7½ min 17 min	7 min 16 min	+ + + + + +
Pasta, medium (macaroni, etc.)	½ lb (225 g) 1 lb (450 g)	14 min 28 min	13 min 26 min	12 min 24 min	+ + + + + +
Pasta, large (lasagna)	1 lb (450 g)	16 min	15 min	14 min	+ + +
Peas	1 lb (450 g)	8 min	7½ min	7 min	+ + +
Peppers (sliced)	1 lb (450 g)	10 min	9½ min	9 min	+ + +
Potatoes, cut up for mashing (whole) (au gratin)	1 lb (450 g) 3 medium 1 lb (450 g)	7½ min 9 min 12 min	7 min 8½ min 11½ min	6½ min 8 min 11 min	+ + + + + + + + +
Rice, natural	½ lb (225 g)	18 min	16½ min	15 min	+ + +
Rice, instant	½ lb (225 g)	6 min	5½ min	5 min	+ + +
Spinach	1 lb (450 g)	8 min	7½ min	7 min	+ + +
Tomatoes, whole (4 medium)	1 lb (450 g)	5½ min	5 min	4½ min	+ + +
Turnip (cubed)	1 lb (450 g)	10 min	9½ min	9 min	+ + +
Zuchinni and summer squash (cubed or sliced)	1 lb (450 g)	9 min	8½ min	8 min	+ + +

TOMATOES ITALIAN STYLE

Servings	1	2
Setting	+++	+++
500 watts	min 4	min 6
600/650 watts	3 3/4	5 1/2
700 watts	3 1/2	5
Standing Time	2	3
Calories	460	
Fat Content	Quite High (40 g)	
Utensil: Round Gratin Dish and Bowl	7 in (18 cm)	9 in (22 cm)
Ingredients		
Medium size tomatoes	2	4
Ground beef	2 oz (60 g)	4 oz (120 g)
Sausage meat	2 oz (60 g)	4 oz (120 g)
Chopped onion	2 tbsp	4 tbsp
Chopped parsley	1 tbsp	2 tbsp
Chopped thyme	1 tsp	2 tsp
Egg yolk(s)	1	2
Whipping cream	1 tsp	2 tsp
Paprika	1/2 tsp	1 tsp
Lemon juice	1 tsp	2 tsp
Pepper	1/4 tsp	1/2 tsp
Salt	1/4 tsp	1/2 tsp

Chop onion, parsley and thyme.

Mix above ingredients with ground beef, sausage meat, cream, egg yolks and seasonings.

Hollow tomatoes and stuff with mixture. Replace tomato tops and arrange tomatoes in gratin dish.

Run tomato pulp through blender to make sauce.

- Prepare all chopped ingredients (ground beef, sausage meat, onion, parsley and thyme).
- Hollow out tomatoes, without piercing skin. Set aside tomato top and reserve tomato pulp for sauce.
- Mix ground beef, sausage meat, onion, parsley and thyme. Add egg yolks, cream and paprika.
- Salt and pepper using half quantities given in recipe.
- Stuff tomatoes with mixture. Cover with tomato top and arrange in a circle in gratin dish.
- Put tomato pulp through blender with lemon juice and the rest of salt and pepper. Pour into bowl.
- Cook both dishes in microwave according to chart instructions.
- Let stand. Serve.

It's better to prepare two medium size tomatoes per person than one very large tomato, as the stuffing will cook more evenly and stay moister.

Tomato and Potato au Gratin

Servings	2	4
Setting	+ + +	+ + +
500 watts	min 12	min 22
600/650 watts	11 1/2	21
700 watts	11	20
Standing Time	3	4
Calories	190	
Fat Content	Very Low (7 g)	
Utensil: Gratin Dish	1/2 qt (0.5 l)	1 qt (1.5 l)
Ingredients		
Medium size tomatoes	2	4
Medium size potatoes	2	4
Chopped onion	2 tbsp	4 tbsp
Chopped garlic	1 tsp	2 tsp
Chopped parsley	1 tbsp	2 tbsp
Whipping cream	2 tbsp	4 tbsp
Grated nutmeg	1/2 tsp	1 tsp
Pepper	1/4 tsp	1/2 tsp
Salt	1/2 tsp	1 tsp

Peel potatoes. Cut into thin slices and set in cold water with lemon juice.

Slice tomatoes. Chop onion, parsley and garlic; grate nutmeg.

Mix cream with onion, garlic, chopped parsley, nutmeg, salt and pepper.

Alternate layers of potatoes, tomatoes and cream mixture in the gratin dish until all ingredients have been used.

- Peel potatoes. Cut into thin slices and set in cold water with a bit of lemon juice.
- Slice the tomatoes.
- Grate nutmeg.
- Chop onion, garlic and parsley.
- Mix cream with onion, garlic, chopped parsley, nutmeg, salt and pepper.
- Drain and dry potatoes well.
- Alternate layers of potatoes, tomatoes, and cream mixture in gratin dish, until all ingredients are used.
- Cover dish with plastic wrap and cook in microwave according to chart instructions.
- Let stand. Serve. A delicious accompaniment for roasted meats, especially pork or lamb.

To keep the vegetables as moist as possible, do not perforate plastic unless in threatens to burst.

Ratatouille

Servings	•4/5	• 6/7•
Setting	+ + +	+ + +
500 watts	min 30	min 45
600/650 watts	28	42
700 watts	26	39
Standing Time	6	9
Calories	300	
Fat Content	Quite Low (25 g)	
Utensil: Pyrex Cooking Dish	2 qts (2 l)	3 qts (3 l)
Ingredients		
Large tomatoes	3	5
Medium zucchini	3	5
Medium eggplant	2	3
Red pepper(s)	1	2
Green peppers	2	3
Large onion(s)	1	2
Garlic buds	4	6
Lemon juice	2 tbsp	3 tbsp
Chopped parsley	3 tbsp	5 tbsp
Chopped thyme	2 tsp	3 tsp
Chopped rosemary	1 tsp	1 1/2 tsp
Olive oil	1/2 tsp	3/4 tsp
Cayenne pepper	1/2 tsp	3/4 tsp
Salt	1 tsp	1 1/2 tsp

Pick lovely fresh vegetables.

Wash vegetables in cold water. Peel eggplant, onion and garlic.

Cut eggplant, zucchini, peppers and onion into slices. Cut tomatoes in sections.

Arrange all vegetables in pyrex dish.

- Select lovely fresh vegetables.
- Wash vegetables in cold water. Peel eggplant, onion and garlic.
- Chop garlic, parsley, thyme and rosemary.
- Cut eggplant, zucchini, peppers and onion into slices. Cut tomatoes into sections.
- Arrange all vegetables in pyrex dish.
- Add garlic, parsley, thyme and rosemary.
- Sprinkle with lemon juice and half the olive oil.
- Add salt and cayenne pepper. Stir.
- Cook in microwave according to chart instructions. Cover for first half of cooking time. Uncover for second half.
- Stir 4 times during cooking process. Turn pyrex dish a quarter turn each time *(see pages 28 and 31)*.
- Sprinkle on the rest of the olive oil 5 minutes before the end of cooking process. Stir gently and check seasoning.
- Let stand. Serve. This ratatouille may be served cold during the summer season.

A lovely simple dish that brings the aroma of summer and sunshine all year.

Zucchini au gratin

Servings	• 1	• 2 •
Setting	+ + +	+ + +
500 watts	min 5 + 4	min 7 + 4
600/650 watts	5 + $3^3/_4$	7 + $3^3/_4$
700 watts	5 + $3^1/_2$	7 + $3^1/_2$
Standing Time	1	2

Calories	210
Fat Content	Low (12 g)

Utensil: Cooking Dish with Steamer *(see p. 19)* and plastic dish or plate

Ingredients

Zucchini, blanched and thinly sliced	1 cup	2 cups
Chopped red pepper	2 tbsp	4 tbsp
Diced or grated cheese	3 tbsp	6 tbsp
Pepper	$^1/_4$ tsp	$^1/_2$ tsp
Salt	$^1/_4$ tsp	$^1/_2$ tsp
Cherry tomatoes to garnish (optional)	1	2

Blanch zucchini as instructed on p. 36.

Steam zucchini in microwave. Dice the red peppers and cheese small.

When zucchini is cooked, sprinkle with cheese and red pepper, cubes. Cooke in microwave to melt cheese.

- Blanch zucchini as instructed on p. 36 and slice thin. If they are, very fresh, slices without peeling them; add 1 minute to first cooking time.
- Arrange zucchini slices on the steamer grill and pour 1/4 cup of water in bottom section. Cover and cook in microwave for first time period on chart.
- While zucchini is cooking, dice the red pepper small; dice the cheese small or use grated cheese.
- Let zucchini stand, then arrange single servings on plates.
- Sprinkle with cheese and decorate with red pepper cubes. Return to microwave for second cooking time on chart.
- Add salt and pepper and serve immediately. (Decorate with a cherry tomato in the middle of each serving if desired.)

Simple, tasty and original, this vegetable dish is a perfect accompaniment for poultry or any other white meat, and for fish.

STEAMED BROCCOLI

Servings	1	2
Setting	+ + + and + +	+ + + and + +
500 watts	min 6 + 1	min 10 + 1 1/2
600/650 watts	5 3/4 + 1	9 1/2 + 1 1/2
700 watts	5 1/2 + 1	9 + 1 1/2
Standing Time	1	2
Calories	230	
Fat Content	Low (17 g)	

Utensil: Microwave Steamer Dish
(see p. 19)

Ingredients

Broccoli	1/2 lb (225 g)	1 lb (450 g)
Butter	1 tbsp	2 tbsp
Whipping cream	1 tbsp	2 tbsp
Lemon juice	1 tsp	2 tsp
Chopped tarragon	1 tsp	2 tsp
Pepper	1/4 tsp	1/2 tsp
Salt	1/4 tsp	1/2 tsp

Break broccoli into flowerets.

Arrange broccoli on top of steaming dish and pour water into bottom section.

Cover before cooking in microwave.

Reduce setting to MEDIUM and cook sauce while keeping broccoli warm in bottom of microwave.

- Break broccoli into flowerets.
- Set broccoli in top of steaming dish.
- For one serving, pour 1/4 cup water into bottom dish; 1/2 cup water for 2 servings, and 1 cup of water for 4 servings.
- Cover and cook in microwave for first time period on chart.
- Let stand at end of cooking time. Prepare sauce. (If oven is equipped with a shelf, you can set broccoli on bottom of oven while sauce cooks on the top shelf.)
- In bowl, mix butter, lemon juice, chopped tarragon and half the salt and pepper. Cook in microwave on MEDIUM for second time period on chart.
- Half way through cooking process, add cream and stir.
- Season broccoli with rest of salt and pepper. Serve with tarragon sauce.

Cooking time of the sauce is purposely short. You could cook it a little longer, but keep an eye on it; the sauce will separate if it boils.

Broccoli Mousse

Servings	•2•	•4•
Setting	+ +	+ +
500 watts	min 5	min 7
600/650 watts	$4^1/_2$	$6^1/_2$
700 watts	4	6
Standing Time	*	*
Calories	180	
Fat Content	Low (12 g)	
Utensil: Individual Ramekins	2	4
Ingredients		
Steamed broccoli	$^1/_2$ lb (225 g)	1 lb (450 g)
Whipping cream	$^1/_4$ cup	$^1/_2$ cup
Egg(s)	1	2
Gelatin Sheet **	2	4
Grated Nutmeg	$^1/_4$ tsp	$^1/_2$ tsp
Pepper	$^1/_4$ tsp	$^1/_2$ tsp
Salt	$^1/_4$ tsp	$^1/_2$ tsp

* Let stand until cold.

** 1 gelatin sheet = 1 tsp of granulated gelatin.

Steam broccoli as directed on p. 206.

Drain carefully. Grate nutmeg.

Run broccoli through blender with cream, eggs, nutmeg, salt and pepper. Add dissolved gelatin and blend once again to a fine creamy texture.

- Steam broccoli as described on p. 206.
- Drain carefully.
- Grate nutmeg and dissolve gelatin *(see p. 35)*.
- Put broccoli in blender with cream, eggs, nutmeg, salt and pepper; process until the mixture is creamy and smooth.
- Add dissolved gelatin and mix once again.
- Pour into ramekins. Cover with wax paper and cook in microwave according to chart directions.
- Let stand and cool. Set in refrigerator until gelatin sets, at least 2 hours.
- Serve in ramekins or unmold by placing ramekins in hot water and turning over on serving dish.

An ideal accompaniment for fish or grilled chicken at a summer feast.

Spinach Burgers

Servings	2	4
Setting	+ + +	+ + +
500 watts	min 8	min 12
600/650 watts	7 1/2	11 1/2
700 watts	7	11
Standing time	5	7
Calories	310	
Fat Content	Low (15 g)	
Utensil: Gratin dish	1 qt (1 l)	2 qts (2 l)
Ingredients		
Thawed spinach	2 cups	4 cups
Whipping cream	2 tbsp	4 tbsp
Grated nutmeg	1/4 tsp	1/2 tsp
Salt	1/4 tsp	1/2 tsp
Canned tomatoes	1 cup	2 cups
Ground beef	4 oz (120 g)	8 oz (240 g)
Egg(s)	1	2
Chopped onion	2 tbsp	4 tbsp
Chopped chervil	1 tbsp	2 tbsp
Soya sauce	1 tbsp	2 tbsp
Tabasco sauce	3 drops	6 drops

Drain spinach well. Add cream, nutmeg and salt.

Break up tomatoes with a wire whisk. Add to ground beef, onion, chervil, eggs, soya and tabasco sauces.

Cover bottom of cooking dish with half the spinach mixture. Spread tomato meat mixture over.

Top with second half of spinach mixture.

- Drain spinach thoroughly.
- Add cream, nutmeg and salt to spinach. Stir.
- Break up tomatoes with wire whisk.
- Add tomatoes to ground beef, eggs, onion and chervil, soya sauce and tabasco sauce. Work this mixture until ingredients are well blended.
- Cover bottom of cooking dish with half the spinach mixture.
- Cover with meat and tomato mixture and top with second half of spinach mixture.
- Cover dish and cook in microwave according to chart directions.
- Let stand. Serve.

A simple family dish that is both tasty and nutritious.

Stuffed Cabbage Leaves

Servings	2	4
Setting	+++	+++
	min	min
500 watts	9	16
600/650 watts	$8^1/2$	15
700 watts	8	14
Standing Time	5	7
Calories	520	
Fat Content	Quite High (47 g)	
Utensil: Use Paper Towels		
Ingredients		
Fresh, unblemished green cabbage leaves	4	8
Chopped green cabbage leaves	1/4 cup	1/2 cup
Sliced carrots	1/2 cup	1 cup
Chopped onion	1/4 cup	1/2 cup
Chopped parsley	2 tbsp	4 tbsp
Chopped thyme	2 tsp	4 tsp
Ground Beef	4 oz (120 g)	8 oz (240 g)
Lard or bacon	3 oz (85 g)	6 oz (170 g)
Smoked sausage	3 oz (85 g)	6 oz (170 g)
Pepper	1/2 tsp	1 tsp
Salt	To taste	

The success of this gastronomical feast depends on the quality and freshness of its ingredients.

Pull off large cabbage leaves, discarding outermost leaves as they are often blemished.

Coarsely chop lard or bacon, smoked sausage, carrots, onion, parsley and thyme.

Stuff cabbage leaves with mixture and roll. Use wooden skewer to prevent unrolling during cooking process.

- This dish can be a gastronomical delight on the condition that all ingredients are fresh and of the best quality.
- Pull off the outer leaves of cabbage. Discard outside leaves as they are often blemished.
- Reserve the most regularly shaped and beautiful leaves for the rolls.
- Chop the rest for the quantities given.
- Remove skin from sausage and excess fat from bacon or lard.
- Coarsely chop lard or bacon, sausage, carrots, onion, parsley and thyme.
- Add ground beef, chopped cabbage, pepper and salt. Stir carefully.
- Stuff cabbage leaves with mixture and roll. Skewer rolls with wooden skewers to prevent unrolling during cooking process.
- Cook in microwave between two sheets of paper towel according to chart instructions. Turn over half way through cooking time.
- Let stand. Serve immediately, with a tomato sauce if desired.

You may wish to present this delicious meal on large cabbage leaves instead of plates for a picnic.

Candied Potatoes

Servings	2	4
Setting	+ + + and + +	+ + + and + +
500 watts	min 8 + 6	min 18 + 8
600/650 watts	$7^1/_2 + 5^1/_2$	$17 + 7^1/_2$
700 watts	7 + 5	16 + 7
Standing Time	5	7
Calories	340	
Fat Content	Quite Low (24 g)	
Utensil: Deep casserole	1 qt (1 l)	2 qts (2 l)
Ingredients		
Small new potatoes	8	16
Butter	3 tbsp	6 tbsp
Chopped garlic	2 tsp	4 tsp
Chopped tarragon	2 tsp	4 tsp
Chopped parsley	1 tbsp	2 tbsp
Pepper	$^1/_2$ tsp	1 tsp
Salt	$^1/_4$ tsp	$^1/_2$ tsp

Peel new potatoes leaving unpeeled 'caps' at both ends for decoration.

Work butter with garlic, tarragon and parsley; add salt and pepper and mix well.

Drain potatoes when cooked. Return with butter spread to microwave set on MEDIUM. Stir often.

- Peel new potatoes leaving unpeeled 'caps' at both ends for decoration.
- Set in casserole with $^1/_2$ cup hot water.
- Cover and cook in microwave set on HIGH for first cooking time on chart.
- Work butter with garlic, tarragon and parsley; add salt and pepper and beat till creamy.
- Drain potatoes at the end of cooking time. Let stand. Return to casserole with butter and garlic mixture.
- Cook in microwave on MEDIUM for second cooking time on chart.
- Stir often during cooking process.
- Serve immediately as main course or to accompany grilled or poached fish.

Such an easy and fast way to prepare a simple dish with special zest and refinement.

VEGETABLE PANCAKE

Servings	1	2
Setting	+ + +	+ + +
500 watts	min 5	min 8
600/650 watts	$4^3/_4$	$7^1/_2$
700 watts	$4^1/_2$	7
Standing Time	2	3
Calories	320	
Fat Content	quite low (17 g)	
Utensil: Round au gratin dish or browning dish	6 in (15 cm)	8 in (20 cm)
Ingredients		
Medium size potatoes	2	4
Medium size carrot(s)	1	2
Medium size onion(s)	1	2
Chopped garlic	1 tsp	2 tsp
Chopped parsley	2 tbsp	4 tbsp
Egg	1	2
Grated cheese	1 tbsp	4 tbsp
Curry	$^1/_2$ tsp	1 tsp
Pepper	$^1/_4$ tsp	$^1/_2$ tsp
Salt	$^1/_4$ tsp	$^1/_2$ tsp

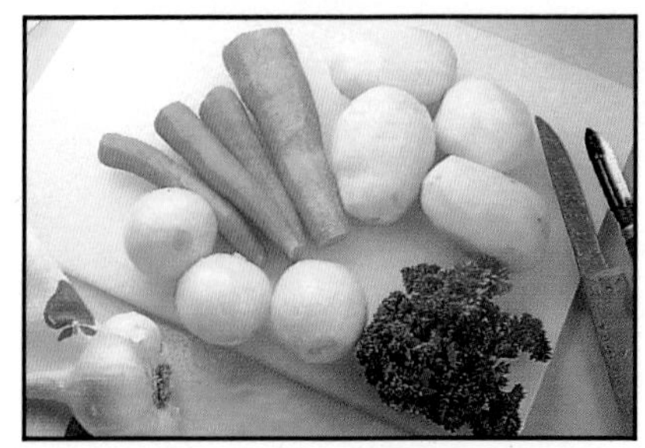

Carefully peel, wash and dry all vegetables.

Grate potatoes, carrots and onions with medium-fine grater.

Put vegetables in bowl and add chopped garlic and parsley, grated cheese, eggs, curry, pepper and salt.

Stir until ingredients are thoroughly blended.

- Carefully peel, wash and dry all vegetables.
- Grate potatoes, carrots and onions medium-fine.
- Place grated vegetables in bowl and add chopped garlic and parsley, grated cheese, eggs, curry, pepper and salt.
- Stir until ingredients are thoroughly blended.
- Shape mixture into large biscuits or pancakes and put in au gratin dish or on browning dish. Cook according to the chart opposite.
- If using browning dish, preheat it *(see page 20)*.
- Rotate dish halfway through cooking time.
- Serve immediately, once standing time has elapsed, with fowl or meat which has been grilled, roasted or even cooked in a sauce.

A truly original and delectable dish fit for a king... and as easy as pie with a microwave oven!

NEW POTATOES WITH SAFFRON

Servings	2	4
Setting	+ + +	+ + +
500 watts	min 9	min 20
600/650 watts	8 1/2	19
700 watts	8	18
Standing Time	3	5
Calories	250	
Fat Content	very low (9 g)	
Utensil: bowl	1 qt (1 l)	2 qt (2 l)
Ingredients		
Small new potatoes	8	16
Lemon juice	2 tbsp	4 tbsp
Powdered saffron	1/4 tbsp	1/2 tbsp
Chopped chives	1 tbsp	2 tbsp
Butter	2 tbsp	4 tbsp
Pepper	1/4 tsp	1/2 tsp
Salt	1/4 tsp	1/2 tsp

Peel, wash and dry new potatoes.

Sprinkle with saffron. Add lemon juice and an equal amount of water.

Stir potatoes several times during cooking. Meanwhile prepare chive butter.

- Peel, wash and dry new potatoes.
- Place in cooking bowl.
- Sprinkle with saffron. Add lemon juice and an equal amount of water.
- Stir to completely coat all potatoes, which will immediately take on lovely red color.
- Cover bowl and cook according to the chart opposite, stirring two or three times during cooking.
- Meanwhile, carefully blend butter with finely-chopped chives, pepper and salt.
- Once potatoes are cooked, drain and place on serving dish. Dot with chive butter and enjoy as soon as it begins to melt.

Nature's simplest vegetable enhanced by two exceptional herbs; saffron and chives! Despite the addition of fresh butter, this dish is nutritious and is easily digested!

LASAGNA

Servings	3	6
Setting	+++	+++
500 watts	min 20	min 30
600/650 watts	19	28
700 watts	18	26
Standing Time	5	7
Calories	480	
Fat Content	average (33 g)	
Utensil: rectangular dish	11 in × 6 × 4	
Ingredients		
Precooked green lasagna noodles	10	20
Minced beef	8 oz (225 g)	16 oz (450 g)
Tomato sauce	1 cup	1 cup
Chopped onion	2 tbsp	4 tbsp
Chopped thyme	1 tsp	2 tsp
Chopped rosemary	1 tsp	2 tsp
Grated cheese	1/2 cup	1 cup
Béchamel sauce	1 cup	2 cups
Grated nutmeg	1 tsp	2 tsp
Pepper	1 tsp	2 tsp
Salt	1 tsp	1 tsp
Olive oil	1 tbsp	2 tbsp

Purchase precooked lasagna or precook it yourself (see pages 37 and 197).

Mix minced meat, onion, thyme, rosemary, salt, pepper and tomato sauce. Prepare bechamel sauce.

Place alternating layers of lasagna, tomato meat mixture, béchamel sauce and grated cheese in pan and repeat process five times.

- Purchase precooked lasagna or precook it yourself *(see pages 37 et 197)*.
- Mix chopped onion, thyme and rosemary with meat.
- Add tomato sauce, salt and pepper. Mix carefully.
- Prepare a traditional béchamel sauce or buy it ready-made. Do not add too much salt. Use grated nutmeg to bring out flavour.
- Line dish with plastic wrap to make lasagna easier to remove after cooking.
- Cover bottom of dish with layer of lasagna; cover with layer of tomato meat mixture, then with layer of béchamel sauce. Sprinkle with grated cheese.
- Repeat layering process 5 times, ending with grated cheese.
- Sprinkle with olive oil.
- Cover with plastic wrap and cook according to the chart opposite. Rotate pan once or twice during cooking.
- Serve immediately, once standing time has elapsed.

The microwave cooks lasagna so well, you'd think it had been invented by an Italian chef!

Antilles-Style Corn

Servings	1	2
Setting	+ + +	+ + +
500 watts	min 7	min 13
600/650 watts	$6^1/2$	12
700 watts	6	11
Standing time	3	5
Calories	390	
Fat content	quite low (21 g)	
Utensil: rectangular Pyrex dish	$^3/4$ qt (0.75 l)	$1^1/2$ qt (1.5 l)
Ingredients		
Fresh corn	2	4
Avocado pulp	3 tbsp	6 tbsp
Butter	1 tbsp	2 tbsp
Crushed chilis	$^1/8$ tsp	$^1/4$ tsp
Lime juice	1 tsp	2 tsp
Salt	$^1/4$ tsp	$^1/2$ tsp
Rum (optional)	1 tsp	2 tsp

If fresh corn is used, cook it in the husk.

Place cobs in dish. Do not add water.

Prepare Antilles Butter by mashing together avocado pulp, butter, chilis, salt, lime juice and rum.

Cream butter into smooth paste. If corn is not cooked in the husk, place $^1/4$ cup water in cooking dish.

- If fresh corn is unavailable, use frozen; cooking time will only have to be increased one or two minutes.
- If fresh corn is used, it is preferable to cook it in the husk.
- Place cobs in Pyrex dish. Do not add water, but cover with plastic wrap.
- Cook according to the chart opposite. Rotate dish halfway through cooking time.
- Meanwhile, prepare Antilles Butter by mashing together avocado pulp, butter, chilis, salt, lime juice and rum. Mix well to form smooth paste. Chill until serving time.
- Let corn stand. Serve with Antilles Butter.

Avocado, chili, lime and rum combine to give a festive creole touch to corn!

DESSERTS

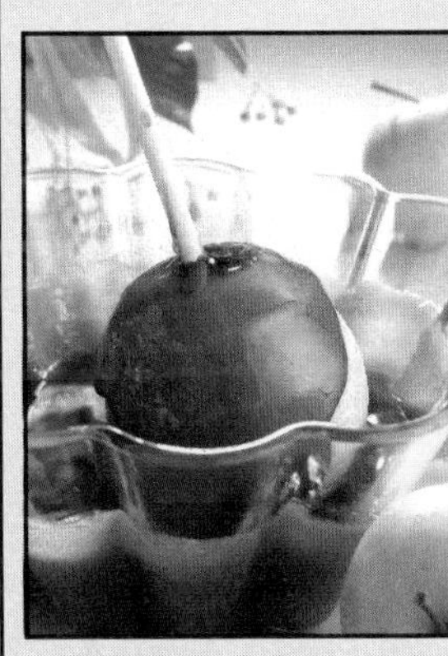

Tips for the Preparation of Desserts

The microwave oven is a terrific tool for gourmands, because you can produce a great variety of desserts and pastries with hardly a failure.

In the microwave, fruits keep their color, flavor and texture; fillings turn out creamy and smooth in a flash; cakes cook evenly and pastry gets crisp; cream sauces seldom separate and chocolate never burns...

Obviously, it's impossible to give a cooking chart for desserts, because they are too numerous and varied and each recipe requires a specific and precise cooking time.

We should mention however that most of your personal and family recipes, as well as most pastry recipes, can turn out very well in the microwave without very much modification.

You can also save time, since desserts cook two to three times faster in the microwave than with the classic equipment.

Some basic points:

— Mousses, custards and any desserts containing cream or eggs should be cooked at half power (MEDIUM).

— Their cooking time will always be brief (a couple of minutes, and sometimes just a matter of seconds).

— They need to be stirred often during cooking.

— Desserts and even pastries are better prepared in individual servings than in larger quantities.

— Sauces can be reheated in the microwave without much risk of curdling or separating.

— As with other foods, you can camouflage the pale color of pie crusts and cakes with appropriate garnishes, and by using some of the tricks that will be pointed out in the following recipes.

— Undercooking is never serious, but overcooking is.

— Microwave ovens are equally convenient for the preparation of hot drinks and cocktails (grogs), and for making jellies and jams.

— Since desserts are by definition sweet, we have included the sugar content per portion for the dessert recipes, along with calorie and fat content.

Chocolate Sauce

Chocolate sauce is definitely one of the basic recipes used most often in dessert recipes.

There are very few people who do not appreciate its luxurious flavor and texture. Whether on a cake or as a filling, as a glaze or with fruit, chocolate sauce always seems to add a delicious note.

The microwave lets you make chocolate sauce easily, quickly and neatly, without messy pots to scrub and without chocolate splatters all over the kitchen walls. The plastic bowl can be cleaned easily under hot running water.

There are many varieties of chocolate sauce, each with its particular special touch. Depending on its ultimate use, you want a sauce that is more or less liquid, more or less sweet, more or less rich, etc. In fact, all your recipes can easily be adapted to the microwave.

We are offering here a particularly sophisticated recipe, which adapts to many purposes, and which can be made lighter or thinner with the addition of a little water before reheating.

For 1 qt (1L) of sauce:
2 slabs of dark semi-sweet baking chocolate
1 1/2 cups water
1/2 cup whipping cream
4 oz (110 g) butter
1/4 tsp salt

Heat the water and the salt for 3 minutes in a bowl. Meanwhile, break the chocolate in small pieces and put it in a 3 qt (3L) bowl.

Pour 1/3, or about 1/2 cup, of the boiling water over the chocolate and put in the microwave on HIGH for:

	min.
500 watts	4
600/650 watts	3½
700 watts	3

At this point, the chocolate will only be partially melted. Put it aside. Mix the cream and the butter in a bowl and put in microwave on MEDIUM for:

	min.
500 watts	3
600/500 watts	2¾
700 watts	2½

Pour the butter-cream mixture into the chocolate

and stir vigorously with a whisk.

Add the rest of the water. It should be lukewarm. Cold water will not blend well with the chocolate and boiling water will make it lumpy.

Beat again with the whisk
and put in the microwave on HIGH for:

	min.
500 watts	2¼
600/650 watts	2
700 watts	1⅚

Stir midway through.

Let stand for 3 minutes. Beat one last time. The chocolate sauce will now be perfectly creamy and smooth.

PEARS "AU CHOCOLAT"

Servings	1	2
Setting	+ + +	+ + +
500 watts	min 5	min 8
600/650 watts	$4^3/_4$	$7^1/_2$
700 watts	$4^1/_2$	7
Standing time	2	3
Calories	340	
Fat content	quite low (15 g)	
Sugar content	quite low (40 g)	
Utensil: shallow dish	$^1/_2$ qt (0.5 l)	1 qt (1 l)
Ingredients		
Pear(s)	1	2
Chocolate sauce	$^1/_4$ cup	$^1/_2$ cup
Lemon	$^1/_2$	1

Choose fresh, sweet juicy pears. Peel them, preferably with a paring knife.

With an apple-corer, carefully remove the core, leaving the stem for decoration.

Prepare chocolate sauce according to the recipe on pages 226-227.

- Choose fresh, sweet, juicy pears.
- Peel them, preferably with a paring knife.
- As you peel, rub the cut surface with lemon to prevent discoloration.
- With an apple-corer, carefully remove the core, leaving the stem for decoration.
- Prepare chocolate sauce according to the recipe on pages 226-227.
- Place pears in cooking dish. Add about $^1/_2$ inch (14 mm) water, preferably preheated.
- Cook according to the chart opposite.
- After standing time has elapsed, place each pear on a dessert plate and top with hot chocolate sauce.
- Serve immediately and enjoy!

Of course, you can prepare peaches, apricots, apples, mangoes, or the fruit of your choice using the same easy recipe!

RED FRUIT COULIS

Servings	2	4
Setting	+ + +	+ + +
500 watts	min 6	min 9
600/650 watts	$5^1/2$	8
700 watts	5	7
Standing Time	*	*
Calories	170	
Fat content	none	
Sugar content	quite low (40 g)	
Utensil: bowl	1/2 qt (0.5 l)	1 qt (1 l)
Ingredients		
Red summer fruit**	1/2 lb (225 g)	1 lb (450 g)
Powdered sugar	1/2 cup	1 cup
Lemon juice	2 tbsp	4 tbsp
Chopped fresh mint (optional)	1 tbsp	2 tbsp

* Until completely cool.

** In culinary jargon, "red fruit" includes all the summer berries. Many of them are in fact red, but others may be purplish or black. Some examples are strawberries, raspberries, gooseberries, black currants, blackberries, bilberries and blueberries.

Pick over and hull fruit; wash and drain carefully.

Place fruit, powdered sugar and lemon juice in blender.

Blend until very smooth.

When the coulis is cooked, press through a sieve.

- Pick over and hull fruit.
- Wash and drain carefully.
- Place fruit, sugar, lemon juice and fresh, chopped mint (if desired) in blender.
- Process until very smooth.
- Pour into cooking bowl and cook according to the chart opposite.
- Strain to remove seeds.
- Stir briskly. Let stand until cool.
- This coulis makes a delicious topping for any dessert or pastry.

A pastry chef is often judged by the quality of his coulis. With this simple microwave recipe, you can become an instant cordon-bleu cook!

STRAWBERRY WREATH

Servings	4	6
Setting	+ + +	+ + +
500 watts	min 15	min 22
600/650 watts	14 1/2	21
700 watts	14	20
Standing Time	*	*
Calories	530	
Fat Content	quite low (16 g)	
Sugar Content	quite high (85 g)	
Utensil: Shallow round dish	8 in. (10 cm)	10 in. (25 cm)
Ingredients		
Strawberries	1 lb (450 g)	1 1/2 lb (675 g)
Brown sugar	1/4 cup	1/3 cup
Cream cheese	1/2 cup	3/4 cup
Egg whites	2	3
Brioche crumbs	1 cup	1 1/2 cups
Gelatin granules	4 tsp	6 tsp

* Until completely cool.

Hull and wash strawberries. Dissolve gelatin as described on page 35.

Break brioche into crumbs. Beat egg whites until stiff but not dry.

Place tumbler in centre of baking dish so that finished cake will be wreath-shaped.

- Hull and wash strawberries.
- Dissolve gelatin in small amount of water, as described on page 35.
- Break brioche into crumbs.
- Beat egg whites until stiff but not dry.
- Blend strawberries to a coarse purée.
- Mix together with cream cheese, brioche crumbs, brown sugar, beaten egg whites and dissolved gelatin.
- Beat vigorously until well-blended.
- Place tumbler in centre of baking dish so that finished cake will be wreath-shaped.
- Pour batter into baking dish; cover and bake according to the chart opposite.
- Cool. Serve topped with Red Fruit Coulis *(see pages 230 and 231)*.

As a simple family dessert or a sophisticated finish to a dinner party, this cake is sure to please!

Caramel

Portions	•4 to 8•
Power Setting	+ + +
500 watts	min 12
600/650 watts	11
700 watts	10
Standing	5

Calories	200
Fat Content	Negligeable
Sugar Content	quite low (46 g)
Utensil: bowl	3 qt (3 l)
Ingredients	
Powdered sugar	1 cup*
Water	1/5 cup*
Lemon juice	1 tbsp
Milk	1 cup

* The proportion of 5 to 1 for sugar and water must be carefully followed in all caramel recipes.

Assemble the ingredients.

Mix the sugar, water and lemon juice.

When the caramel reaches a boil add the milk.

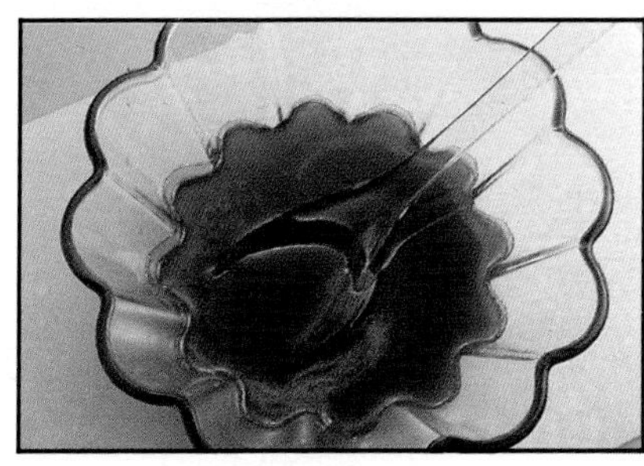

Pass through a fine sieve before using.

- Mix the powdered sugar, the water and the lemon juice in a bowl.
- Put in the microwave on HIGH for the time directed on the chart.
- As soon as the caramel reaches a boil, add the hot milk and beat vigorously.
- Pass through a fine sieve, and use the caramel on any dessert, such as the apple in the photograph opposite.

Caramel is one of the most delicate and messiest preparations you can produce in the kitchen.

It's even worse than chocolate sauce, leaving you with a pot that is so hard to clean you might be tempted to throw it in the garbage.

This is another case of the microwave coming to the rescue, making it possible to produce caramel without the slightest damage to the kitchen equipment.

It's just a question of technique and organization...

PEACHES "AU CARAMEL"

Servings	2	4
Setting	+ + +	+ + +
500 watts	min 5	min 8
600/650 watts	$4^1/2$	$7^1/2$
700 watts	4	7
Standing Time	3	4
Calories	400	
Fat Content	low (12 g)	
Sugar Content	average (73 g)	
Utensil: Pyrex casserole	$^1/2$ qt (0.5 l)	1 qt (1 l)
Ingredients		
Peaches	2	4
Caramel sauce (see page 234)	$^1/2$ cup	1 cup
Shelled peanuts	2 tbsp	4 tbsp
Fresh chopped mint	2 tbsp	4 tbsp
Hot water	$^1/2$ cup	1 cup

Pour hot water into casserole and add peaches.

Once cooked, peaches are easy to peel.

Cut in half and remove stones.

Place peaches on serving plate. Top with caramel sauce. Sprinkle with chopped peanuts and fresh mint.

- Pour hot water into casserole.
- Add peaches.
- Cook according to the chart opposite.
- Peel, cut in half and remove stones.
- Prepare caramel sauce according to recipe on page 254.
- Chop peanuts and fresh mint.
- Place peach halves on serving dish.
- Top with caramel sauce.
- Sprinkle with chopped peanuts and mint.
- Serve immediately.

These peaches "au caramel" can be kept in the refrigerator and reheated for a few minutes in the microwave just before serving.

ALASKA OMELETTE

Servings	1	2
Setting	+ + +	+ + +
500 watts	min $2^1/_2$	min 4
600/650 watts	$2^1/_3$	$3^5/_6$
700 watts	$2^1/_6$	$3^1/_3$
Standing Time	1	2

Calories	260	
Fat Content	very low (5 g)	
Sugar Content	low (46 g)	
Utensil: serving plate	1	
Ingredients		
Egg whites	2	4
Powdered sugar	2 tbsp	4 tbsp
Chocolate shavings	1 tbsp	2 tbsp
Coffee ice cream	1 scoop	2 scoops
Fresh mint	for decoration, if desired	

Beat egg whites until stiff.

Blend in granulated sugar and chocolate shavings.

Pour into serving dishes and cook according to the chart.

- Beat eggs whites until stiff.
- Blend in powdered sugar and chocolate shavings. Beat slightly longer.
- Pour into serving dishes.
- Cook according to the chart opposite.
- Place scoop of ice cream in centre of cooked "omelette".
- Decorate if desired with sprig of fresh mint and enjoy immediately.
- This dessert can be prepared with any kind of ice cream or sorbet.
- The contrast between the hot egg whites and cold ice cream is what makes this dessert so appealing.

Gourmets will quickly notice the similarity between this Alaska omelette and a Norwegian omelette. The main difference between the two is that here, the ice cream is added at the end.

In fact, if the ice cream was placed under the eggs at the beginning of cooking in the microwave oven, it would melt before the omelette was done.

Softening Ice Cream

We have already pointed out that the microwave is a perfect companion to the freezer.

We have all experienced the simple process of taking something out of the freezer, popping it into the microwave and producing perfect results with little or no effort.

But here is another little-known but very convenient application of the microwave...

You take for instance, a strawberry sherbet out of the freezer...

You guests are waiting for dessert, while you are struggling to form the sorbet into attractive balls... but the sherbet is too hard and crumbles!

Put the container of sherbet or ice cream in the microwave, on MEDIUM, for:

	min.
500 watts	1½
600/650 watts	1¼
700 watts	1

You can now scoop out beautifully shaped balls, at just right temperature for serving.

Be careful to serve right away, or the sherbet will get too soft.

Preparation of Pastry

To be perfectly honest, the microwave oven can very quickly turn out pastry with all the features of conventially-made pastry... flaky and delicious, with one exception; the crust does not turn golden brown.

As a result, you have to use some special little tricks to mask the pale color. To begin with, let us start with a frozen ball of pastry.

Take the pastry ball out of the freezer. Grease the pie plate and sprinkle flour on the work surface.

Also dust the rolling pin with flour, and roll out the pastry to the approximate size of the pie plate.

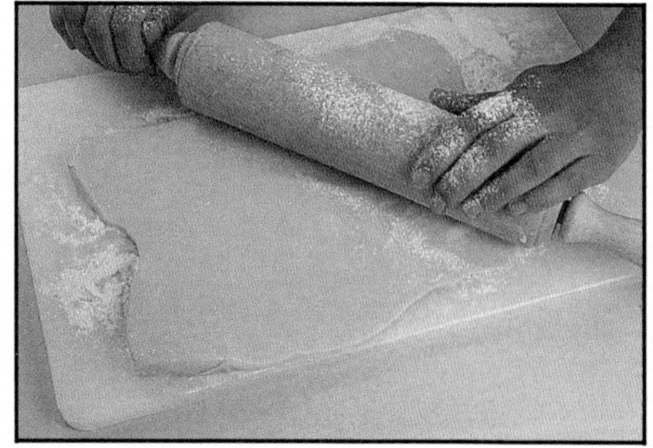

Line the pie plate with pastry, pressing it carefully into the bottom of the pan; be careful not to tear the dough. Trim the edges. Prick all over the bottom of the pastry with a fork so that it stays flat during cooking.

Now comes the strategic moment to tint the pastry. The best solution is to use chocolate sauce (see recipe on pages 228 and 229). Use a pastry brush to apply the chocolate sauce to all visible parts of the crust. During cooking, the chocolate sauce will give an appetizing color to the crust. You could also replace the chocolate sauce with fruit jelly (red currant or apricot).

Another solution, although we do not really recommend it, is to tint the crust with food coloring.

Apple Pie

Servings	4	6
Setting	+ + +	+ + +
500 watts	min 17	min 22
600/650 watts	16	21
700 watts	15	20
Standing Time	4	6
Calories	360	
Fat Content	low (15 g)	
Sugar Content	quite low (35 g)	
Utensil: microwave pie plate	8 in. (20 cm)	10 in. (25 cm)
Ingredients		
Pie pastry	7 oz (200 g)	10 oz (300 g)
Medium-sized apples	4	6
Powdered sugar	4 tbsp	6 tbsp
Butter	2 tbsp	3 tbsp

Prepare pastry as indicated on page 241.

Peel and core apples and slice thinly.

Arrange apple slices in concentric circles, sprinkling each layer with sugar and dotting with butter.

- Roll out pastry. Line pie plate. Apply coloring as shown on preceding page.
- Peel and core apples.
- Cut apples in half, then slice thinly.
- Arrange slices in concentric circles in pastry-lined pan.
- Make several layers until all slices have been used, sprinkling each layer with sugar and dotting with butter.
- Bake according to the chart.
- Serve immediately after standing time has elapsed as this pie, while delicious cold, is even better hot.

Use this recipe for pear, plum or apricot pies, too. Of course, when using strawberries, raspberries or other fragile berries, the crust should be pre-cooked and filled when cool.

CLAFOUTIS

Servings	•4/5	• 6/7•
Setting	+ + + then + +	+ + + then + +
500 watts	min 4+6+14	min 6+9+21
600/650 watts	4+5 1/2 +13	6+8 1/2 +20
700 watts	4+5+12	6+8+19
Standing Time	6	4

Calories:	360	
Fat Content	low (14 g)	
Sugar Content	average (48 g)	
Utensil: Pyrex au gratin dish	1 1/2 qt (1.5 l)	2 qt (2 l)
Ingredients		
Cherries, preferably fresh	2 cups	3 cups
Eggs	4	6
Powdered sugar	4 tbsp	6 tbsp
Flour	4 tbsp	6 tbsp
Milk	1 cup	1 1/2 cups
Salt	1/3 tsp	2/3 tsp

Choose fresh, juicy cherries. Pour milk into Pyrex measuring cup and heat in microwave.

Beat eggs and sugar in bowl. Add flour and salt. Stir.

Add milk to egg mixture in a thin stream, beating vigorously.

Pit cherries.

- Choose fresh, juicy cherries.
- Pour milk into Pyrex or plastic measuring cup and set microwave on HIGH for the first length of time indicated in the chart opposite
- Meanwhile, beat eggs and sugar in a bowl.
- Add flour and salt. Mix well.
- When milk is hot, slowly add to egg mixture in a thin stream, beating vigorously to avoid curdling.
- Place bowl in microwave and cook at medium for the second length of time indicated in the chart. Stir twice during cooking.
- Pit cherries.
- Beat mixture in bowl once more. Pour into gratin dish.
- Place cherries in dish and arrange them attractively.
- Cover with greaseproof paper and microwave at MEDIUM for the last length of time indicated in the chart.
- After standing time has elapsed, serve clafoutis hot or cold.

This special microwave clafoutis requires a bit of fuss, but the delicious result will make it all worthwhile.

FRUIT CAKE

Servings	•5/6	• 8/9•
Setting	+ + +	+ + +
500 watts	min 12	min 18
600/650 watts	11	$16^{1}/_{2}$
700 watts	10	15
Standing Time	5	7
Calories	400	
Fat Content	low (14 g)	
Sugar Content	quite high (63 g)	
Utensil: loaf pan	10 in × 4	12 in × 4
Ingredients		
Flour	7 oz (200 g)	10 oz (300 g)
Eggs	2	3
Butter	5 oz (140 g)	7 oz (200 g)
Powdered sugar	6 oz (170 g)	9 oz (250 g)
Assorted candied fruit	4 oz (120 g)	6 oz (170 g)
Salt	$^{1}/_{4}$ tsp	$^{1}/_{2}$ tsp
Yeast	1 pkg	1 pkg

* 10 po × 4 = 25 cm × 10
** 12 po × 4 = 30 cm × 10

Carefully weigh all ingredients. Soften butter.

Blend softened butter and powdered sugar in bowl. Whip.

Add flour, eggs, salt and yeast.

Add chopped candied fruit. Line pan with plastic film.

- Soften butter 1 minute on MEDIUM heat.
- Chop candied fruit.
- Carefully weigh all ingredients.
- Blend softened butter and sugar in a bowl. Whip.
- Add flour, eggs, salt and yeast.
- Knead, until mixture becomes a soft, elastic dough.
- Add chopped candied fruit and knead again to ensure even distribution.
- Line pan with plastic wrap to make cake easy to remove after cooking.
- Fill pan with dough. Smooth surface and cook according to the chart opposite.
- Enjoy hot or cold, plain or topped with a fruit coulis *(see page 230)* or a chocolate sauce *(see pages 226 and 227)*.

A little secret regarding the last recipe of this collection: we had to remake this cake three times before finding the right cooking time! However, now you are assured of a successful result.

Coca-Cola

Index

A

B

C

M

N.O.P.

Q.R.

S

T

U.V.W.X.Y.Z.

Notes

The Author wishes to acknowledge
and thank the following:

Yvonne Pelard,

Eugénie, Ahn and Hippolyte Dard,
Félicie Myotte,
Armelle Pelard,
Edouard Maître
Katia Wilson,

Guy Brière
Elisabeth Schlittler
Denis Gignac
Jean-Claude Côté
Pierre Chapleau
Michèle Noiseux
Jean-Pierre Patenaude
Jill Bauch
Robyn Bryant
and Robert M. Béliveau

whose help and assistance
have contributed to the sucessful
presentation of this book.